Executive Function Difficulties in Adults

100 Ways to Help Your Clients
Live Productive and Happy Lives

Stephanie Moulton Sarkis, PhD

Published by
PESI Publishing & Media
PESI, Inc.
3839 White Ave
Eau Claire, WI 54703

Cover Design: Amy Rubenzer
Layout: Amy Rubenzer & Bookmasters
Editing: Jenessa Jackson

Proudly printed in the United States of America

ISBN: 9781683730989

PESI
Publishing
& Media
www.pesipublishing.com

About the Author

Stephanie Moulton Sarkis, PhD, is the bestselling author of five books: *10 Simple Solutions to Adult ADD: How to Overcome Chronic Distraction & Accomplish Your Goals*; *Natural Relief for Adult ADHD: Complementary Strategies for Increasing Focus, Attention, and Motivation With or Without Medication*; *Adult ADD: A Guide for the Newly Diagnosed*; *ADD and Your Money: A Guide to Personal Finance for Adults with Attention Deficit Disorder*; and *Making the Grade with ADD: A Student's Guide to Succeeding in College with Attention Deficit Disorder*.

Dr. Sarkis is an American Mental Health Counselors Association Diplomate and Clinical Mental Health Specialist in Child and Adolescent Counseling. She is a National Certified Counselor and Licensed Mental Health Counselor, maintaining a private practice in Tampa, Florida. She is also a Florida Supreme Court certified family mediator and civil circuit mediator. She is the founder of Sarkis Institute, which specializes in treatment of ADHD, anxiety, and chronic pain disorders. Dr. Sarkis is a blogger for *Psychology Today* and *The Huffington Post*. In 2001, she received an American Psychological Association Outstanding Dissertation Award for her research on executive functions and their impact on pediatric comorbid ADHD.

Dr. Sarkis has been published numerous times, including in the *Journal of Attention Disorders*, the *National Psychologist*, and *The ADHD* Report. She has presented at numerous venues, including ACA, CHADD, ICP, and PESI. She has made several media appearances, including CNN, ABC News, Fox News, Sirius Satellite Radio, *Woman's Day*, and First Business Television. Dr. Sarkis is featured in the book *The Gift of Adult ADD* By Lara Honos-Webb, Ph.D. Dr. Sarkis created the Moulton-Farnsworth Scholarship for college students with ADHD. Dr. Sarkis' website is www. stephaniesarkis.com

Contents

Introduction

WHY THIS WORKBOOK IS NEEDED AND WHO IT IS FOR

Executive function (EF) difficulties occur in many different disorders. Executive dysfunction can occur in disorders such as attention deficit hyperactivity disorder (ADHD), anxiety, post-traumatic stress disorder (PTSD), depression, autism spectrum disorder (ASD), dementia, age-related memory decline, chronic traumatic encephalopathy, and traumatic brain injury (TBI). How many people are affected by executive function difficulties? Approximately 4.4% of people in the United States, or roughly 11 million people, meet diagnostic criteria for ADHD (Kessler, et al., 2006). More than 4.8 million people in the U.S. have ASD (Centers for Disease Control, 2016). Age-related memory decline, including executive function difficulties, are an inherent part of getting older – in 2014 there were 34 million U.S. residents aged 65 and older – and by the year 2030 one in five U.S. citizens will be 65 and older (Colby and Ortman, 2015). Many of the individuals described above are seeking techniques to use to combat these problems in lieu of psychotropic medication, or treatments to use alongside their medication.

This workbook addresses this large segment of the population, many of whom are seeking answers as soon as they make their initial phone call to you. There is a great deal of misinformation online, and non-reputable treatments abound – and some can cost people a great deal of money and time. This workbook provides reputable, researched treatments all in one place.

When we took on our clinician licenses, we agreed to provide the best quality of care to our clients/patients. We achieve this by giving individualized treatment – acknowledging that each client is unique in their needs, challenges, hopes, fears, and dreams. This workbook helps you tailor that individual treatment. The happiest day of a clinician's life is when a client tells you that they are doing well enough to not need to come in as much – let's get more people to that place, together.

This workbook provides:

- Easy-to-understand descriptions and diagrams of the causes of executive function impairment;
- A chart describing various instruments used in the assessment and evaluation of executive function performance;
- Treatments that have a substantial amount of research backing them as being effective and valid;
- A breakdown of cognitive-behavioral therapy (CBT) techniques, which have the most evidence compared to any talk therapy technique for success in improving executive function impairment;
- Instructions on how to practice mindfulness meditation, one of the most effective forms of treatment for executive function issues;

- Information on the effectiveness of accommodations for those in college and the workplace, along with detailed checklists for your client, including steps you need to take to write an effective accommodations request letter;

- Detailed information on how sleep disorders impact executive function performance;

- Changes to diet and how they impact executive function performance;

- Research showing that movement/exercise is one of the most effective forms of treatment for executive function impairment;

- Techniques for improving social skills when clients have difficulty processing nonverbal cues and have issues with reconstituting information;

- Tips for making day-to-day living easier and more productive for your client;

- Future directions for executive function research and treatment.

WHY THIS WORKBOOK IS DIFFERENT

While there are books and workbooks available on ADHD, anxiety, depression, ASD, TBI, and other brain issues, there was not a workbook for clinicians working with adults focusing on one of the commonalities of these disorders: executive function impairment. Another difference with this workbook is that it is written for you, the clinician – with worksheets for you and your clients. In addition, this workbook focuses mainly on non-medication treatments – treatments that are versatile in that clients can use them whether or not they take psychotropic medication.

HOW TO USE THIS WORKBOOK

This workbook provides you, the clinician, with the research and details behind each worksheet and activity, instructions for use with your clients, and how to integrate the activity into your clients' treatment. The activities in the workbook can be done in sequential order, or in the order that is most appropriate for your client – it is all in your control. The activities are stand-alone and simplified – your client will not need any extra tools or information, or need to spend any money to complete them successfully. The activities also provide enough of a challenge for your client to be motivated – but not too much of a challenge as to be a roadblock. Above all, the activities are interesting, different, and fun – a must-have when working with clients who have executive function impairment.

As you go through the activities and information in this workbook, remember that the best treatments for your client are ones that:

- Are low-cost

- Are easy access

- Do not require equipment

- Do not require training

- Are evidence-based

As you read through the workbook, you may find some exercises and worksheets that blend well with your practice and your clients, and some that you need to adjust to meet your and your client's needs. Remember that clients (and clinicians) are each unique.

CHAPTER 1

Critical Components

WHAT ARE EXECUTIVE FUNCTIONS?

Executive functions (EF) refer to a set of cognitive processes such as selective attention, working memory, set-shifting, planning, and inhibitory control, which are governed by the **frontal lobe** of the brain, particularly the **dorsolateral prefrontal cortex** (DLPFC). The DLPFC is only found in primates, like humans and apes. The DLPFC plays an important role in our ability to organize and process information, make decisions, plan ahead, manage time, regulate moods, store information, learn from mistakes and consequences, and get motivated to start and complete tasks (Brown, 2009; Barkley, 2005). Together, these metacognitive processes make up what are known as the executive functions. In other words, think of the executive functions as doing things similar to what an executive does at a company: they take in, process, and distribute information. Their primary functions are to inhibit and self-regulate behavior.

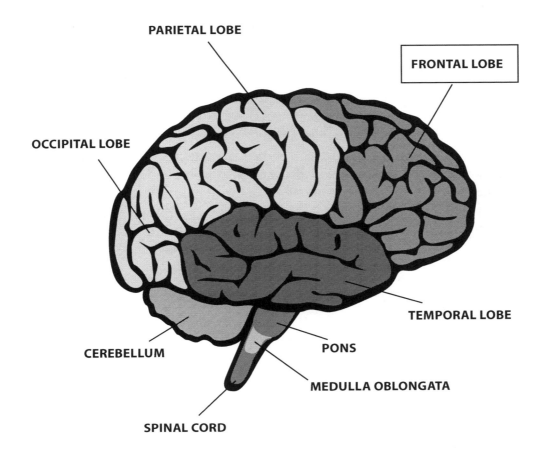

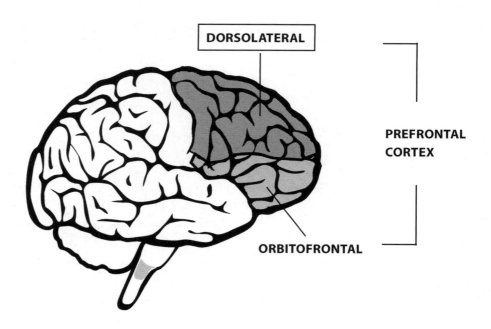

INHIBITION AND SELF-REGULATION

When you have disorders like ADHD, PTSD, anxiety, or a traumatic brain injury (TBI), the executive functions can become impaired. Impairment in executive functions (or *executive dysfunction*) can cause forgetfulness, difficulty getting motivated, an inclination to lose items, a tendency to interrupt others, hyperfocusing (which causes difficulty switching tasks), and can even cause mood swings.

Moreover, when a person has executive dysfunction, it is difficult for him or her to *self-regulate* and inhibit behaviors. Self-regulation is the ability to get back on task, without needing any external redirection or reminders. Behavioral inhibition is the ability to stop and think about how one is going to respond to a particular stimulus. It allows a person to think through something without becoming distracted – it controls for "interference" in the environment. It's like a stop sign pops up reminding a person to hold a thought instead of interrupting, or to think about whether a choice is in a person's best interest. With executive dysfunction, that stop sign tends to pop up a little late or not at all. In this chapter you will learn about the specific executive functions and what happens when they are not working properly.

EXECUTIVE FUNCTION TASKS

As you just read, the main purpose of executive functions are to inhibit and self-regulate behavior. These functions include:

- Working Memory
- Time Management
- Emotion Regulation
- Cognitive Flexibility
- Planning

- Forethought
- Learning from Consequences
- Organization
- Reconstitution of Information

Next you will learn about each of these executive functions, and how the dysfunction of each impacts your clients' lives. For a screening instrument regarding each of the executive functions, please see Appendix B in the back of the workbook.

Working Memory

There are three types of memory: short-term, long-term, and working memory. Short-term memory is used to remember where you parked your car at the grocery store. Once you locate your car after shopping, your brain dumps that information. You no longer need that information for any useful purpose. This is one of the reasons it is difficult to get accurate witness accounts after a crime – your brain dumps a lot of the details (Lacy and Stark, 2013). Long-term memory is used to hold your families' names and your address – information you need to recall during your lifetime. Working memory is where you hold, process, and manipulate information. When a person is engaging working memory, they are storing information into short-term memory and using it for a task.

The working memory process functions in the following cycle:

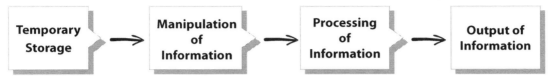

For example, on the Mini-Mental State Examination, a client is asked to spell the word "WORLD" backwards. This is a working memory task. First, the clinician's instructions are held in the client's short-term memory. The client then visualizes that word, and starting from the end, says each letter out loud. This task is a multi-step process, and can be very difficult for people with executive dysfunction to complete. Anywhere along this four-step process, individuals with executive dysfunction can get tripped up; they may fail to even hold the task instructions in temporary storage. This is why it is important that people with working memory difficulties are allowed accommodations in the classroom, such as extended time on tests. It is also why it is important to break tasks down into bite-sized pieces for people with executive dysfunction – only giving one instruction at a time and writing the instructions down. You will learn more about accommodations in Chapter 6.

EXERCISE ## Quick Test of Working Memory

For a quick test of working memory, ask your client to spell the word "WORLD" backwards, or to conduct "serial sevens" (subtracting 7 from 100, and then continuing to subtract 7 from each new number all the way down). Be mindful of clients who have a reading or math disability. If they have a reading disability, have them conduct serial sevens. If they have a math disability, have them do the word task.

Time Management

Time management is an executive function that has a great impact on success in the workplace and on activities of daily living. The client with time management difficulties may get their appointment time wrong, even when you call the day ahead to confirm; may show up late for their appointment; and may ask if the appointment time is over yet. When clients have time management difficulties, they tend to have difficulties:

- Estimating how long it takes to complete a task or reach a destination
- Overestimating or underestimating how much time has passed
- Determining when an event happened (month/year)
- Arriving on time to events and appointments, even when they try their hardest to be punctual and it is important to them
- Realizing on which tasks to expend extra effort, and which tasks they can do until their work is "good enough"
- Judging how long it will take to drive somewhere – especially forgetting to take into account rush hour
- Reading an analog (non-digital) clock

In addition to the frontal lobe of the brain, time estimation and time management is governed by the temporal lobe of the brain.

EXERCISE   # Quick Test of Time Management

Set a timer for a "non-standard" amount of time, such as 2 minutes or 3 minutes (don't do 5 minutes, as that is a "standard" guess). Do not tell the client the time you set, and have them take off or turn over any timepiece. Continue on with the session. When the timer goes off, ask the client how much time has passed. People with time management difficulties will usually grossly overestimate or underestimate the time.

Emotion Regulation

When you have good emotion regulation, you feel like you are on an "even keel." Nothing really tips you too far in either direction of your mood. You also tend to have an *internal locus of control*. This means that you feel pretty secure and solid — it's like you have an invisible shield around you. You let daily annoyances just "bounce off" of you. If you have difficulty with emotion regulation, you tend to have more of an *external locus of control*. Things really get to you, and it's difficult for you to pull yourself out of a bad mood.

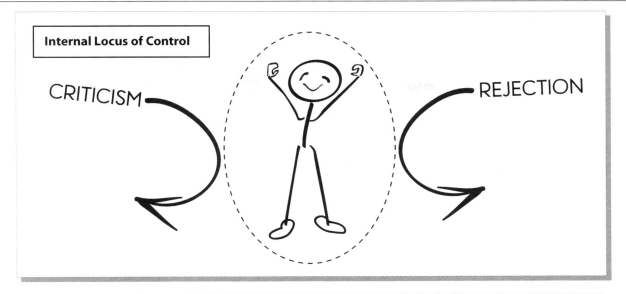

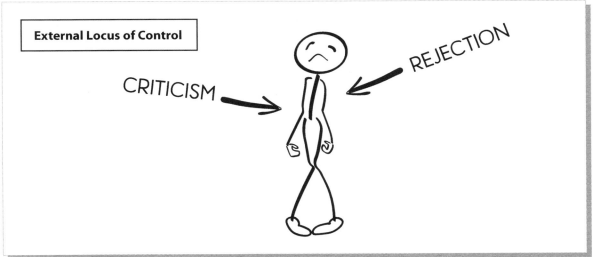

Having difficulty with emotion regulation means you tend to get frustrated more easily, and sometimes you show it through socially inappropriate behavior – like throwing something or cursing. You tend to also get more "ramped up" than your friends in social situations – resulting in your voice volume getting louder and louder. A friend may tell you to lower your voice, but the volume creeps right back up again.

EXERCISE   ## Quick Test of Emotion Regulation

Ask your client to draw a flat line on a sheet of paper. This is your client's baseline. Now have them talk about the events of their week. For every event, have your client put a dot above the line for how happy or content they were and a dot below the line for how mad, frustrated, or sad they were. Now take a pencil and connect the dots. See how much the line varies from baseline. The more jagged the line, with high peaks and low valleys, the more your client may be having difficulty regulating emotions.

Cognitive Flexibility

Cognitive flexibility is the ability to switch from one thought to another, or to contemplate more than one thought at a time. A fundamental part of learning is to hold different thoughts at one time, such as rules and concepts of rules. Therefore, people with cognitive *inflexibility* find it very difficult to learn new concepts when the rules are changed – resulting in frustration and difficulty meeting demands at school or in the workplace. For example, you are playing the card game Hearts with your friends. It is announced that you will be playing Crazy Eights every other hand. You need to switch from one set of rules to another very quickly. The brain has to keep up with all the new rules and know when to switch to the other set of rules. It can become very time-consuming, frustrating, and costly when you have executive dysfunction.

EXERCISE

Quick Test of Cognitive Flexibility

In order to do a quick test of cognitive flexibility, you need to have a task in which you are changing rules quickly. In this variation of the Knock-Tap Test you may discover quickly if your client has issues with cognitive flexibility.

First, have your client seated across from you at a table. Give your client the instruction that when you knock on the table, they respond by tapping their flat palm on the table. When you tap your flat palm on the table, they respond by knocking – in other words, the exact opposite response. Do this five times in a random sequence, with a few seconds between each response.

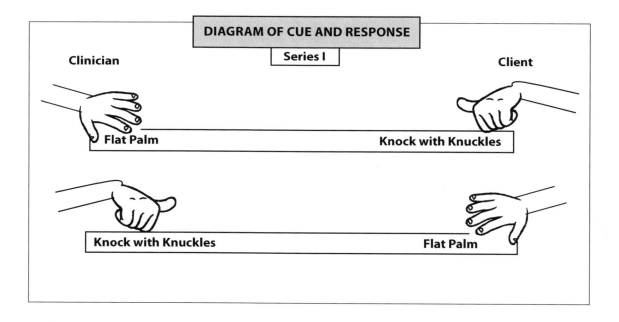

In the next step, you are changing up the rules. When you knock, the client taps the table withn their side fist. When you tap on the table, your client is instructed to not respond. When you tap the table with your side fist, your client knocks on the table. Do this five times, in a random sequence, with a few seconds between each response.

This exercise is testing how your client adapts to different rules, and the addition of a rule requiring inhibited response (not performing a behavior). People with executive dysfunction, particularly difficulties with cognitive flexibility, will have difficulties holding new rules and inhibiting responses.

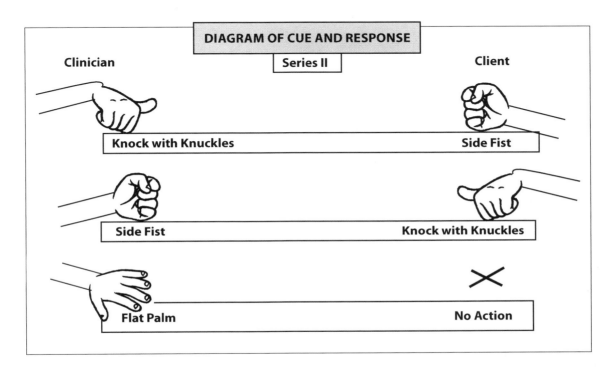

DIAGRAM OF CUE AND RESPONSE

Series II

Clinician | Client

Knock with Knuckles | Side Fist

Side Fist | Knock with Knuckles

Flat Palm | No Action

Planning

Planning is the "conscious or deliberate specification of a sequence of actions aimed at achieving some problem goal" (Borowski and Burke, 1999, p. 257). When you engage in planning, you consider the effects of your actions on your goals and also on long-term time frames. For example, you are planning to go to your office's annual picnic on Saturday, and you have signed up to bring potato salad. A week before the picnic, you write on your "to do" list that you need to pick up potato salad from the deli the morning of the picnic. The morning of the picnic, you get up a little early so you have time to run to the store. You realize what might happen if you forget the potato salad – you haven't fulfilled your obligation, and your office may be annoyed or upset. It may even reflect poorly on you as an employee. Not wanting to upset people can be a powerful motivator!

However, if you have difficulty with planning due to deficits in executive functioning, you may not write down that you need to pick up potato salad. You build in extra time to your schedule to stop by the deli, but you vaguely recall you were supposed to bring something. So you run in and just pick up the first thing you see. Now not only are you late to the picnic, but you also have no potato salad. When you have impairments in planning, you tend to lack formed goals and have difficulty comprehending how being prepared helps you in the long-term. This then results in you waiting until the last minute to complete tasks.

EXERCISE   # Quick Test of Planning

For a quick test of planning, create a task where your client must decide what steps to take to accomplish the task. Have a series of index cards with big decisions written on them, such as:

- Buying a car
- Going to college
- Going on a cruise

Make sure the topics aren't emotionally loaded – avoid writing "getting married" or "having kids." Have your client pick a card. It is now up to them to write down or tell you the steps involved. For example, the steps for "buying a car" would involve:

- Seeing how much money you have to buy a car
- Researching what cars have the best ratings
- Looking online to see what cars are available
- Test driving cars
- Bargaining with car dealerships

Forethought

Forethought involves thinking ahead before taking action. You play out scenarios in your mind before making a decision. This is very closely related to the executive function of planning, which you just read about in this chapter. If you have difficulties with forethought, it is a challenge for you to predict what might happen if you pick choice A or choice B. For example, let's say you have the choice of skipping work or showing up. If your forethought process is working well, you think to yourself, "Skipping work sounds really good right now. But if I skip work, I'm missing a big meeting – and that may get me in trouble." A person with poor forethought ability may think, "Skipping work sounds really good. I'm going to do it." With forethought impairment, you may act before thinking, and choose the "path of least resistance" when making decisions. Poor forethought ability can also lead to you having difficulty playing strategy-related games, like chess. With chess, you need to think about what might happen if you move your chess piece to a certain location; and then think again about what would happen if you move another piece. So instead, you just move your chess piece without thinking it through, and you end up losing.

EXERCISE

Quick Test of Forethought

Any strategy-related game can be helpful for testing forethought. A quick strategy-related game you can do with just paper and pencil is called "dots and boxes".

You start out with nine dots drawn on a sheet of paper, like this:

You and your client each take turns connecting two unjoined adjacent dots. The player who completes the fourth side of a box earns a point and gets another turn. The player puts his initial in the completed box. Play continues until all boxes are completed. The player with the most completed boxes wins.

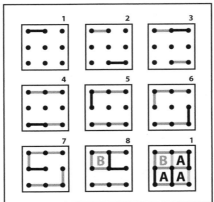

In this game, you are observing how your client thinks ahead to plan their next move. You have to take into account not only your next move, but also how your opponent might respond. If you have poor forethought, you continually make errors that result in you falling further behind in the game.

Learning from Consequences

You keep making the same errors and still get surprised at the unfavorable outcome. Your memories of your previous errors and consequences eventually may kick in, but it's too late – leaving you frustrated at your apparent inability to learn from your mistakes. This illustration describes how your brain works when you are learning from consequences:

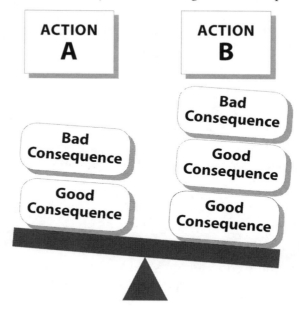

You realize clear consequences for each of your choices. When you are comparing choices, you can pick the best option for the future by looking at which option had the best consequences to it. When you have difficulties with learning from consequences, your brain weighs your actions differently:

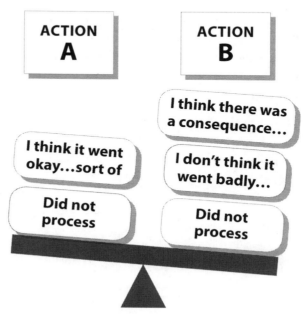

You have difficulties processing consequences to actions, so it's a real challenge to compare two courses of action. You don't have a clear delineation or memory of "good consequences" or "bad consequences." This means that you're not really sure which choice you should make in the future.

EXERCISE

Quick Test of
Learning of Consequences

In this quick test, get two small animal figurines and two cups. Place the figures and cups on the table. Use the following script:

"This is a story about (Animal 1) and (Animal 2). One day, (Animal 1) went out for a walk. Before he left, he put his pet (Animal 2) under this cup. (Put Animal 2 under one of the cups, and walk Animal 1 out of sight.) While (Animal 1) was gone, (Animal 2) decided to play a trick, and hide in the other cup. (Move Animal 2 under the second cup). After his walk, (Animal 1) comes home. Under which cup will he look for (Animal 2) first?"

If a person's ability to learn from consequences is intact, they will say cup 1, because that is where (Animal 1) originally left it. If a person has difficulties with learning from consequences, they will say cup 2. This is because the brain is having difficulty linking action to consequence.

Organization

Your client may try to keep things organized, but they just can't. Your client tells you they spend all day organizing their home office, and it is messy by the next day – or even the next hour. It can be very frustrating and disheartening. Difficulties with organization don't just apply to things and papers – they also apply to organizing your ideas for an outline. Outlines are all about categorizing and using a numbered system. You also use the concept of *hierarchies* to make an outline. For example, if you are writing a paper about animals, your outline may look like this:

I. Animals
  A. Dogs
    1. Dalmatian
    2. Corgi
  B. Cats
    1. Siamese
    2. Bengal
  C. Birds
    1. Cardinal
    2. Blue Jay

But if you have difficulties with organization, you may jump all over with your ideas. You think of your siamese cat and then remember your neighbor has a dalmatian. You jump from topic to topic. This is, in part, due to the fact that it is much easier for individuals with executive dysfunction to create a "visual" outline as opposed to a Roman-numeral "linear" outline. In order to create such visual outlines, there are apps such as Mindjet Maps that help you draw a flow chart of ideas. For example, the outline above would look like this instead:

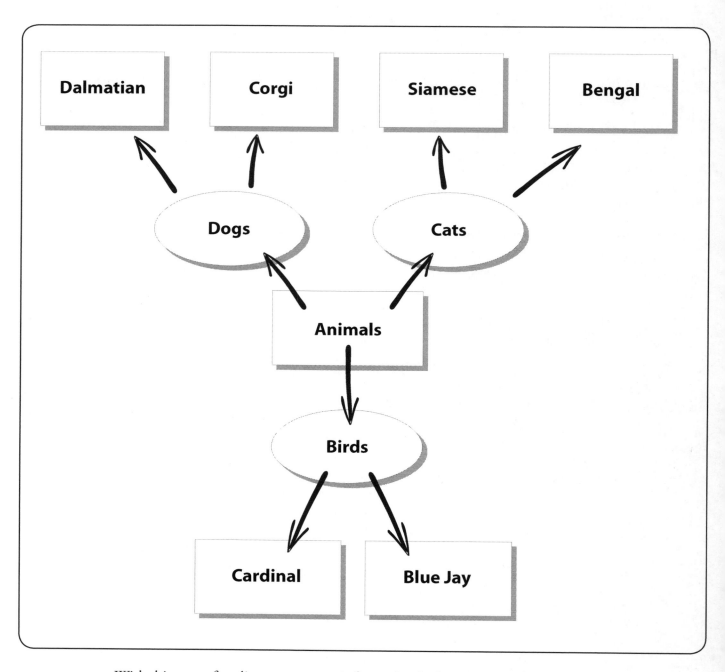

With this type of outline, you can see information laid out in a non-linear fashion – just the way a brain characterized by executive dysfunctioned likes to take in information. Using different colors and shapes also helps the brain separate items into categories.

EXERCISE

Quick Test of Organization

Give your client a set of index cards with the following words written on each card:

Animals	Mammals	Birds	Insects
Dog	Cat	Parrot	Cockroach
Finch	Human	Monkey	Spider
Grasshopper	Fly	Cockatiel	Robin

Ask your client to organize the cards in a hierarchical fashion. It should resemble something like this:

Animals

Mammals	**Birds**	**Insects**
Dog	Parrot	Cockroach
Cat	Cockatiel	Spider
Human	Robin	Grasshopper
Monkey	Finch	Fly

If an animal is unknown due to cultural differences, do not count that against the client. This quick test gives you an idea of the organizational processes involved in the brain – how information is broken down into parts.

Reconstitution of Information

If you have issues with reconstitution of information, you have difficulties taking a message and putting it back out again in the correct format. Your client's spouse tells them they need to pick up milk at the store. He comes home from the store with eggs. An argument ensues about how your client's spouse doesn't feel your client cares about what she has to say. Your client's friend calls and asks if she can meet for dinner at 7 pm tonight. Your client puts 8 pm in their calendar. At 7:30 pm your client gets a call from their friend, wondering why she hasn't shown up yet. This difficulty in understanding messages can create a great deal of stress in a relationship and in friendships.

Think of reconstitution of information like the game "Telephone" you played when you were a kid. A message was passed from kid to kid, all the way down the line from beginning to end. The message at the end was usually different than the initial message. Something gets garbled along the way.

When you have issues with reconstitution of information, there is an issue with how information is processed. This means that when you output it (tell someone else), the message is not the same.

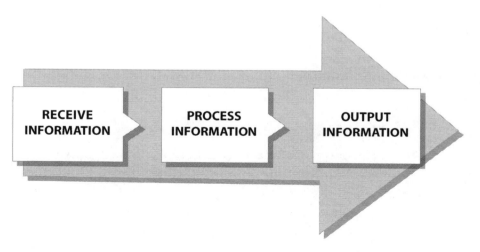

A better way to process information is to have it put in written or typed format. For example, if a coworker asks you to complete part A of a project, you can respond with, "Could you shoot that in an email to me? I appreciate it." Then you have a written record you can rely on, instead of your memory. Having written documentation also means if you have any questions about what your coworker said, you don't need to ask them over and over – the information is right there in the email. It is also helpful to repeat things back to people to make sure you understood them correctly.

Difficulties with reconstitution is one reason why multistep directions are difficult for people with executive dysfunction to process correctly. Give one direction at a time, and write the instructions down.

EXERCISE

Quick Test of Reconstitution of Information

Tell your client a list of three directions:

1. Go to the store.
2. Buy a gallon of milk.
3. Pay with a credit card.

Immediately ask your client the three instructions. Continue with your interview.

After five minutes and ask your client the instructions again. Then near the end of your interview, ask for a final time.

If your client has difficulties with reconstitution of information, you will see that some instructions are skipped and some are misinterpreted.

"Buy a gallon of milk" may be repeated back as "Buy a carton of eggs," as the brain understands the base concept: "buy X amount of Y."

You may also find that "credit card" is replaced with "cash" or "debit card."

CHAPTER 2 Executive Function Impairment

There are many disorders that are characterized by executive function (EF) deficits. In this chapter we'll discuss the disorders that are most commonly affected by (EF) executive dysfunction, including attention deficit hyperactivity disorder, autism spectrum disorder, traumatic brain injury, learning disabilities, and chronic traumatic encephalopathy, among several others. For each disorder, you will learn the predominant EF issues at hand, as well as the disorder's prevalence, age of onset, symptoms, causes, treatment, and prognosis. You'll discover the risk factors and protective factors that help determine whether a person will have executive dysfunction and to what extent. This workbook provides forms for your client's first visit, and the importance of getting a good family history, as many of the disorders you will learn about in this chapter are genetic. Additionally, there is an intake evaluation form to help you better organize the information you get from your client. Finally, you will see what assessments are available for measuring EFs.

Executive dysfunction plays a role in the following disorders:

- ADHD
- Autism Spectrum Disorder
- Traumatic Brain Injury (especially of the frontal lobes)
- Generalized Anxiety Disorder
- Major Depressive Disorder
- Persistent Depressive Disorder (Dysthymia)
- Bipolar Disorder I and II
- Borderline Personality Disorder
- Post-Traumatic Stress Disorder
- Oppositional Defiant Disorder
- Learning Disabilities
- Chronic Pain
- Cognitive Disorders
    - Alzheimer's Disease
    - Pick's Disease (frontotemporal dementia)
- Chronic Traumatic Encephalopathy

The following are handouts you can give directly to clients.

Attention Deficit
Hyperactivity Disorder (ADHD)

PREDOMINANT EXECUTIVE FUNCTION ISSUES

ADHD involves issues with virtually every executive function: planning, organization, working memory, cognitive flexibility, learning from consequences, reconstitution of information, forethought, and time management.

PREVALENCE

ADHD impacts 4.4% of the U.S. population, or approximately 11 million people (Kessler et al., 2006). Worldwide, the prevalence of ADHD is 3% to 6% (Kessler et al., 2011).

AGE OF ONSET

According to *DSM-5®* (American Psychiatric Association, 2013) diagnostic criteria, symptoms must be present before the age of 12.

SYMPTOMS

There are three subtypes of ADHD: inattentive, hyperactive/impulsive, and combined. Symptoms of the inattentive type include:

- Difficulty with organization
- Difficulty sustaining attention to tasks that require sustained mental effort
- Difficulty paying attention to details
- Difficulty with time management
- Losing items frequently

Symptoms of the hyperactive/impulsive include:

- Interrupting
- Difficulty staying seated when it is expected
- Having "inner restlessness"
- Blurting out answers to questions
- Difficulty waiting turns or standing in line

If you meet the diagnostic criteria for both the inattentive subtype and the hyperactive/impulsive subtype, you have the combined subtype. To meet criteria for each subtype, you need to have five out of nine symptoms if you are 17 or older, or six out of nine symptoms if you are 16 or younger.

CAUSE

ADHD is a highly heritable disorder such that if a parent carries the genes for ADHD, there is a 72-88% chance that the child will inherit the genes (Larsson et al., 2013; Rietveld et al., 2004). Several genes associated with ADHD have been identified, and there are hundreds of gene variations found in children with ADHD that are not found in controls (Elia et al., 2010; Guan et al., 2009; Rietveld et al., 2004). Environment plays a much smaller role than genetics in ADHD (Larsson, Chang, D'Onofrio, and Lichtenstein, 2013).

TREATMENT

Stimulant medication and cognitive-behavioral therapy (CBT) have been found to be effective in the treatment of ADHD, with both treatments combined being more effective than either treatment alone (Pelham et al., 2014). Non-stimulant medication is also a treatment option, although when compared to stimulant medication, the latter has been found to be more efficacious (Faraone and Glatt, 2010). Effective non-medication treatment options, besides CBT, include exercise, Omega 3-6-9, and mindfulness meditation. Stimulant medication remains the most thoroughly researched treatment for ADHD and also is the most effective (Purushothaman, 2013).

PROGNOSIS

Early intervention and treatment can greatly reduce the impact of ADHD symptoms on self-esteem and quality of life (Surman et al., 2013; Coghill, 2010). For example, treatment with stimulant medication has been found to decrease the risk of substance abuse or not increase it at all in several studies (Chang et al., 2013; Molina et al., 2013; Wilens, 2004). Symptoms last into adulthood, but hyperactivity and impulsive symptoms may morph into "inner restlessness" due to maturation of the frontal lobes of the brain.

Autism Spectrum Disorder (ASD)

PREDOMINANT EXECUTIVE FUNCTION ISSUES

In ASD, the most prevalent executive function issues include problems with reconstitution of information, planning, emotion regulation, cognitive flexibility, and organization.

PREVALENCE

About 1 in 68 (1.5%) of children in the U.S. meet diagnostic criteria for ASD (Centers for Disease Control, 2016). This equates roughly to 4.8 million people in the U.S.

AGE OF ONSET

Symptoms can be present from birth. Some cases of ASD are first noticed when a child is not acquiring single word speech by the age of one year and phrase speech by the age of 18 months.

SYMPTOMS

Symptoms of ASD include lack of verbal communication, lack of eye contact, difficulty with reciprocal conversation, difficulty with eye contact, difficulty understanding abstract speech (metaphors), repetitive behaviors and rituals, and echolalia. There are three levels or types of ASD, from mild to severe.

CAUSE

Autism spectrum disorder is highly heritable. There is no evidence to suggest autism is caused by vaccines. In fact, several studies have found that there is absolutely no known correlation.

TREATMENT

There are currently no medications for ASD that are approved by the U.S. Food and Drug Administration. Available treatments include behavior therapy, a structured environment, and parental support. Early intervention is essential.

PROGNOSIS

Early intervention is key to outcome. For Type I ASD, it is possible for adults to maintain employment and supported independent living.

Frontal Lobe Traumatic Brain Injury (TBI)

PREDOMINANT EXECUTIVE FUNCTION ISSUES

If the TBI is in the frontal lobes, a variety of executive function difficulties may be present: organization, reconstitution of information, working memory, forethought, planning, time management, emotion regulation, and cognitive flexibility.

PREVALENCE

Every year at least 1.7 million TBIs occur in the United States, across all age groups (Faul, Xu, Wald, and Coronado, 2010).

AGE OF ONSET

TBIs can occur at any age, though they more often occur in the following circumstances: in childhood; among those who work in a manual labor profession; among those who play contact sports; and in older adults who are at greater risk of falling. TBIs are also more common among males.

SYMPTOMS

Symptoms of a traumatic brain injury include:

- Poor judgment
- Lack of insight
- Impulsivity
- Lack of motivation
- Inappropriate comments
- General changes to personality and behavior

CAUSE

Accidents are the most common cause of TBI, including falling and motor vehicle accidents.

PREVENTION

While it is difficult to avoid some forms of head injury, it is important that individuals playing sports, especially high contact sports or sports with high elevation, wear helmets.

TREATMENT

Treatment at the point of injury is essential. Later treatment includes occupational therapy, use of computer applications to improve working memory function, and cognitive medications.

PROGNOSIS

Prognosis of frontal lobe TBI is highly dependent on the severity of injury and promptness of treatment.

Generalized Anxiety Disorder (GAD)

PREDOMINANT EXECUTIVE FUNCTION ISSUES

Individuals with GAD can have difficulty with emotion regulation, organization, reconstitution of information, and cognitive flexibility.

PREVALENCE

Approximately 18.1% of the U.S. population, or 40 million adults, qualify for a diagnosis of GAD (Kessler, Chiu, Demler, and Walters, 2005).

AGE OF ONSET

The median age of onset for GAD is 30 years, with many cases beginning in the early 20s.

SYMPTOMS

GAD symptoms include:

- Excessive worrying
- Muscle tension
- Insomnia
- Being easily fatigued
- Difficulty concentrating or mind going blank

CAUSE

While stress can exacerbate anxiety symptoms, GAD is highly heritable.

PREVENTION

Since GAD is highly heritable, it is important to be aware of symptoms in childhood and begin treatment as soon as possible.

TREATMENT

Cognitive-behavioral therapy has been found to be effective for GAD, along with antidepressant and anxiolytic medications.

PROGNOSIS

With effective treatment, the prognosis for people with GAD is good to excellent.

Major Depressive Disorder (MDD)

PREDOMINANT EXECUTIVE FUNCTION ISSUES

EF issues in MDD include difficulties with emotion regulation, cognitive flexibility, working memory, planning, and forethought.

PREVALENCE

Approximately 6.7% of the U.S. population, or 15 million adults, meet the diagnostic criteria for MDD (Center for Behavioral Health Statistics and Quality, 2016).

AGE OF ONSET

The average age of onset is in the mid-20s, but symptoms can appear at any age.

SYMPTOMS

Symptoms of MDD include:

- Depressed mood most of the day, nearly every day
- Anhedonia
- Excessive feelings of guilt
- Sensation of weighted limbs
- Fatigue or loss of energy
- Rapid amount of weight gain or weight loss
- Insomnia or hypersomnia
- Suicidal ideation
- Agitation or psychomotor retardation
- Difficulty concentrating

CAUSE

Depression is highly heritable. In addition, people with MDD experience a low level of dopamine, serotonin, and norepinephrine in the brain.

PREVENTION

It is essential to pick up on symptoms as early as possible, as some may even occur in childhood.

TREATMENT

Antidepressant medication is the first-line treatment for depression. Once symptoms are under control, cognitive-behavioral therapy has been found to be effective. Non-medication interventions include exercise and mindfulness meditation.

PROGNOSIS

With continued treatment and attention to possible recurrence of symptoms, the prognosis for people with MDD is fair to good, depending on the severity of each recurrence. Recurrence rates are particularly high.

Persistent Depressive Disorder (Dysthymic Disorder) (PDD)

PREDOMINANT EF ISSUES

Executive function issues in PDD include problems with working memory, time management, emotion regulation, and cognitive flexibility.

PREVALENCE

PDD occurs in 1.5% of U.S. adults (Kessler, Chiu, Demler, and Walters, 2005). This equates to approximately 4.8 million people.

AGE OF ONSET

Age of onset can occur at any time, with symptoms most present in adults.

SYMPTOMS

Symptoms of PDD include:

- Depressed mood for at least two years
- Feelings of guilt or worthlessness
- Insomnia or hypersomnia
- Low energy or fatigue
- Low self-esteem
- Poor appetite or overeating
- Poor concentration

CAUSE

PDD is highly heritable. Symptoms can also be exacerbated by stressful situations or by grief.

PREVENTION

The best prevention of worsening PDD is early intervention through medication, cognitive-behavioral therapy, and other treatments.

TREATMENT

Cognitive-behavioral therapy and antidepressant medications are the most effective treatments for PDD.

PROGNOSIS

With adherence to treatment, symptoms can reduce in severity and intensity.

Bipolar Disorder I and II

PREDOMINANT EF ISSUES

Executive function issues in bipolar disorder include difficulties in learning from consequences, organization, and emotion regulation.

PREVALENCE

The amount of people who experience bipolar disorder I or II is 4.4% of the U.S. population, or 14.3 million people (Wittchen, Mhlig, and Pezawas, 2003).

AGE OF ONSET

The average age of onset for bipolar disorder is 25.

SYMPTOMS

Symptoms of bipolar disorder I include mania. Mania is characterized by:

- Not needing to sleep
- Pressured speech
- Impulsive spending
- Poor decision-making

In bipolar II, hypomania is exhibited instead of mania. Hypomania is less intense than mania, and does not include psychotic features.

CAUSE

Bipolar disorder I and II are highly heritable.

PREVENTION

Each time a person with bipolar disorder goes through a manic phase, a phenomenon known as "kindling" occurs. This means that each time a person cycles, the severity increases and onset time shortens. Therefore, early diagnosis and treatment are essential.

TREATMENT

Mood-stabilizing medication is the first-line treatment for bipolar disorder. Antidepressant medication and antipsychotic medication may also be prescribed.

PROGNOSIS

With treatment, prognosis is fair to good. Without adherence to treatment, the prognosis is poor, due to kindling.

Borderline Personality Disorder (BPD)

PREDOMINANT EXECUTIVE FUNCTION ISSUES

Executive function issues in BPD include problems with cognitive flexibility, planning, forethought, and emotion regulation.

PREVALENCE

Borderline personality disorder (BPD) is found in approximately 1.6% of the U.S. population, or approximately 5.2 million people (Lenzenweger, Lane, Loranger, and Kessler, 2007).

AGE OF ONSET

BPD cannot be diagnosed until the age of 18, according to the *DSM-5®* (American Psychiatric Association, 2013). Some symptoms may be present in childhood and adolescence.

SYMPTOMS

Symptoms of BPD include instability in interpersonal relationships, frantic efforts to avoid abandonment, intense anger, impulsive behavior, idealizing and devaluing others and the self, lacking a sense of self, and suicidal behaviors.

CAUSE

Though there is no known cause of BPD, it occurs more often when there is a familial history of BPD and when there has been a history of trauma or abuse, particularly sexual abuse (Infurna et al., 2015).

PREVENTION

There is no known prevention for BPD, save for children of parents with BPD receiving counseling as soon as possible.

TREATMENT

Dialectical Behavior Therapy (DBT) is the first line treatment for BPD. DBT treatment includes cognitive-behavioral and mindfulness meditation components. Antidepressants may also be prescribed.

PROGNOSIS

Due to the inherently pervasive nature of personality disorders, the prognosis for BPD is fair to poor due to lack of adherence to treatment.

Post-Traumatic Stress Disorder (PTSD)

PREDOMINANT EXECUTIVE FUNCTION ISSUES

In PTSD, executive function issues include problems with working memory, time management, emotion regulation, cognitive flexibility, planning, forethought, and reconstitution of information. In cases where PTSD is comorbid with a traumatic brain injury (TBI) involving the frontal lobe, such as in a veteran population, EF dysfunction is amplified.

PREVALENCE

PTSD impacts 3.5% of the U.S. population (Kessler, Chiu, Demler, and Walters, 2005). This equates to approximately 11.4 million people in the U.S.

AGE OF ONSET

The age of onset for PTSD depends on the age when a traumatic event was experienced. In the *DSM-5*®(American Psychiatric Association, 2013), there are now diagnostic criteria not only for adult PTSD, but also for preschool-onset PTSD. Onset of PTSD symptoms can occur six months to years after a traumatic event.

SYMPTOMS

Symptoms of PTSD include a foreshortened sense of one's future, hypervigilance, flattened or "numb" affect, flashbacks, avoidance of places or things that remind a person of the trauma, separation anxiety, and nightmares.

CAUSE

The cause of PTSD is experiencing a trauma that either threatened the life or safety of a person, or witnessing a trauma that threatened the life of or killed another person.

PREVENTION

Prevention of worsening PTSD symptoms includes immediate aftercare in the form of supportive psychotherapy. "Debriefing" for first responders who experienced a trauma is no longer recommended due to the chances of retraumatizing other responders.

TREATMENT

Treatment for PTSD includes cognitive-behavioral therapy, eye movement desensitization and reprocessing therapy, clinical hypnosis, and support animals.

PROGNOSIS

With continuing treatment, prognosis is fair to good. Prognosis is very dependent upon a person's proximity to the trauma, whether loved ones were injured or killed in the trauma, and immediacy of treatment.

Oppositional Defiant Disorder (ODD)

PREDOMINANT EXECUTIVE FUNCTION ISSUES

Children with ODD have been found to have particular difficulties with EF tasks of learning from consequences, planning, and emotion regulation, particularly with negative emotions (Jiang, Li, Du, and Fan, 2016).

PREVALENCE

ODD impacts 10.2% of the U.S. population (Nock, Kazdin, Hiripi, and Kessler, 2007). This equates to approximately 33.1 million people.

AGE OF ONSET

The age of onset for ODD is in childhood or adolescence. If symptoms occur into adulthood and increase in severity, an individual may meet diagnostic criteria for antisocial personality disorder.

SYMPTOMS

Symptoms of ODD include vindictive behavior, holding grudges, picking fights, stealing items of low monetary value, and purposely annoying others. If a child begins to engage in law-breaking behaviors, they may then qualify for a diagnosis of conduct disorder (CD).

CAUSE

Children with ODD have a higher level of cortisol, a stress-producing hormone, in their blood. There is also evidence that ODD is a highly heritable disorder.

PREVENTION

Providing structure, guidelines, and immediate and appropriate consequences to a child with ODD helps decrease the chances of continuing symptoms later in life.

TREATMENT

ODD treatment may include prescription of stimulant medication to help with the impulsivity related to ODD. Cognitive-behavioral therapy has also been found to be effective.

PROGNOSIS

With continuing behavioral intervention, the prognosis is good to excellent.

Learning Disabilities (LDs)

PREDOMINANT EXECUTIVE FUNCTION ISSUES

Predominant executive function issues in learning disabilities include deficits in working memory, cognitive flexibility, organization, and reconstitution of information.

PREVALENCE

LDs occur in 9.7% of the U.S. population, or approximately 31.5 million people (Altarac and Saroha, 2007).

AGE OF ONSET

Severe LDs are usually first noticed in early elementary school. Milder LDs may not be "caught" until a child's natural compensation techniques are no longer able to meet the level of learning complexity.

SYMPTOMS

In a reading disorder such as dyslexia, an individual may not see letters when reading, or letters may appear reversed. They may also not follow a standard "Z" eye-tracking pattern across the page. If a person has a math LD, they may reverse numbers either when viewing a math problem or when transcribing it onto paper.

CAUSE

Some LDs appear to be an issue with the brain's frontal lobe not communicating well with the visual cortex. Learning disabilities are heritable, and they can also be caused by brain damage.

PREVENTION

There is no known prevention of learning disabilities. Early intervention is key.

TREATMENT

There is no known medication treatment for learning disabilities. The most common treatment involves adapting the learning environment to suit the individual's needs. For example, individuals with dyslexia tend to process information better if it is in an audio format. An accommodation for school or work can be "get books in audio format."

PROGNOSIS

With accommodations in place at school and at home, and with a career that adequately shields a person with LD from tasks that the brain has difficulty processing, prognosis is good to excellent.

Chronic Pain

PREDOMINANT EXECUTIVE FUNCTION ISSUES

Executive function issues among individuals with chronic pain include deficits in working memory, time management, and emotion regulation.

PREVALENCE

Pain is a public health crisis that affects over 50 million people in the U.S. (Bauer et al., 2016; Stanos et al., 2016), with chronic unrelenting pain occurring in 30.7% of those cases (Bauer et al., 2016).

AGE OF ONSET

Chronic pain does not discriminate – it affects people of all ages. A quarter of all adolescents experience chronic pain. Adolescent chronic pain usually presents as headaches, abdominal pain, or musculoskeletal pain. Experiencing chronic pain in adolescence is more likely to result in chronic spine pain and fibromyalgia in adulthood (Ali et al., 2016). Overall, the chances of experiencing chronic pain increase with age.

SYMPTOMS

People with chronic pain describe it as either "dull" or "sharp" pain. Dull pain presents as an unremitting ache, while sharp pain presents as a "stabbing" sensation. Referred pain also occurs, wherein one part of the body is injured or inflamed, but the pain expresses itself in another part of the body. For example, people experiencing ear infections may feel pain in their teeth and/or jaw.

CAUSE

The most common causes of chronic pain are congential medical abnormalities (i.e., present at birth), cancer, arthritis, accidents (including work-related accidents and motor vehicle accidents), viruses, and autoimmune disorders. Autoimmune disorders include fibromyalgia, chronic fatigue syndrome, Lyme disease, and lupus. Phantom limb pain affects 98% of amputees.

PREVENTION

It is difficult to prevent chronic pain. Stringent safety regulations in the workplace, particularly with manual labor occupations, greatly reduces the risk of accidents. If there is a family history of arthritis, preventive use of medication may lead to fewer arthritis symptoms later.

TREATMENT

The first-line treatment for pain generally involves non-steroidal anti-inflammatory drugs (NSAIDS). This includes acetylsalicylic acid (Aspirin), ibuprofen (Advil), and naproxen (Aleve). NSAIDS are available via prescription and over-the-counter. Corticosteroids (anti-inflammatories) may be prescribed, such as Cortisone, Prednisone, and Prednisolone. For more severe pain (such as post-operative pain), opioids such as codeine, fentanyl, morphine, and oxycodone are prescribed. Antidepressants and anticonvulsants have also been found to help with some chronic pain symptoms.

With regard to non-medication treatment, psychoeducation about the nature of pain, the importance of self-care, and adherence to a treatment regimen have been effective. In addition, exercise, mindfulness meditation, cognitive-behavioral therapy, and autogenic training have shown effectiveness.

PROGNOSIS

With optimum treatment, chronic pain sufferers report a reduction in symptoms. Rarely is there a full elimination of symptoms, although this differs depending on the origin of the chronic pain.

Cognitive Disorders

PREDOMINANT EXECUTIVE FUNCTION ISSUES

Cognitive disorders are associated with deficits in virtually all of the executive functions: working memory, time management, emotion regulation, cognitive flexibility, planning, forethought, learning from consequences, organization, and reconstitution of information. These executive function deficits worsen over time.

ALZHEIMER'S DISEASE

PREVALENCE

Approximately 5.4 million people in the U.S. have Alzheimer's Disease (AD) (Alzheimer's Association, 2016).

AGE OF ONSET

Age of onset for AD is typically in the 50s or 60s, but some cases have been diagnosed as early as in the 40s.

SYMPTOMS

Symptoms of AD are gradual in the beginning, such as forgetting where items are usually stored, forgetting acquaintances' names, and having difficulty finding the words for objects. With time, there appears to almost be a reversal of acquired skills in that development appears to be going backwards. Forgetting how to tie one's shoes is followed by forgetting how to feed oneself and subsequently by forgetting how to use the bathroom.

CAUSE

AD is highly heritable. In addition, there is some evidence that a buildup of tau proteins in the brain may be, in part, one of the causes.

PREVENTION

At this point, there is no known proven preventative measure. However, some individuals with a genetic predisposition to AD have started taking cognitive medications on a prophylaxis basis.

TREATMENT

Treatment focuses on plateauing or minimizing symptoms. Cognitive medications may also be prescribed for mild to moderate AD. Three medications prescribed for AD are Aricept (donepezil), Exelon (rivastigmine), Namenda (mementine), and Razadyne (galantamine).

PROGNOSIS

Even with treatment, the overall prognosis for AD is poor. Medication may temporarily slow the progression of symptoms, but overall cognitive decline continues to occur.

PICK'S DISEASE

PREVALENCE

Four out of every 100,000 U.S. citizens may receive a diagnosis of Pick's Disease (or frontotemporal dementia) in their lifetime (Onyike and Diehl-Schmid, 2013).

AGE OF ONSET

The age of onset for Pick's Disease is usually between 40 to 60 years of age, but it has been diagnosed as early as 20 years of age.

SYMPTOMS

Symptoms of Pick's Disease can be found in language and in behavior. There is a rapid decline of acquired language and in activities of daily living, which is more rapid than is seen in AD.

CAUSE

Pick's Disease involves a rapid shrinking of the frontal and temporal anterior lobes of the brain. It is a highly heritable disorder.

PREVENTION

There is no known prevention for Pick's Disease. There are genetic tests available that can determine if a person is at risk for developing the disorder.

TREATMENT

The purpose of treatment is to minimize symptoms. Cognitive medications are available, such as those prescribed for AD – Razadyne (galantamine), Exelon (rivastigmine), and Aricept (donepezil).

PROGNOSIS

Due to the rapid progression of Pick's Disease, prognosis is poor. The average length of time from onset of symptoms to death is four years, which is a more rapid decline than found in AD (Rascovsky, et al., 2006).

Chronic Traumatic Encephalopathy (CTE)

PREVALENCE

Chronic Traumatic Encephalopathy, which is a degenerative brain disease, is more prevalent when there is a greater risk of head injury, such as in football or extreme sports. There is not a known prevalence statistic at this time.

AGE OF ONSET

Age of onset correlates with age of repetitive head injury. For example, CTE symptoms occur about 12 to 16 years after the start of a boxing career.

SYMPTOMS

Symptoms of CTE include depression, confusion, personality changes, executive dysfunction, impulsive behavior, and suicidality (Gavett, Stern, and McKee, 2011).

CAUSE

Concussions, specifically repetitive concussions, are the primary cause of CTE. Cerebral atrophy occurs, along with a loss of neurons, scarring of brain tissue, neurofibrillary tangles, and hydrocephalus (Lucke-Wold et al., 2014; Graham and Gennareli, 2000).

PREVENTION

Avoiding high-contact sports and wearing a helmet when engaging in these sports is essential.

TREATMENT

There is no known treatment for CTE at this time.

PROGNOSIS

The prognosis for CTE is poor. CTE leads to a much higher risk for suicide than the general population.

PROTECTIVE AND RISK FACTORS FOR EF ISSUES

Executive function impairment impacts people in different ways, depending on the underlying cause. As you read previously in this chapter, there are a variety of disorders that involve EF impairment. However, there are protective factors that may, at least to some extent, protect the brain from executive dysfunction, while there are also risk factors that increase the chances of developing deficits in EF.

PROTECTIVE FACTORS

Protective factors are those that help decrease the chances of acquiring EF difficulties. These protective factors can be genetic or environmental.

High Intelligence Quotient

Intelligence Quotient (IQ) has not been found to be correlated with EF performance (Antshel et al., 2010). This means an individual can have an average to high intelligence quotient (IQ) and still have significant EF impairment. In one study, adults with high IQ with and without ADHD were given a battery of executive function assessments. High IQ adults with ADHD had more difficulties on seven executive function assessments than high IQ adults without ADHD (Antshel et al., 2010). There may be some advantages if a person with ADHD does have a high IQ. They may be better able to formulate compensation techniques, and learn social cues and subtleties that help individuals successfully ask for assistance from others.

Parents' Education Level

The higher your parents' education level, the more likely you are to have developed better executive functions (Ardila, Rosselli, Matute, and Guarjardo, 2005).

Higher Socioeconomic Status

Children from a middle-class socioeconomic (SES) background scored better on tests of executive function than children from a working-class SES background (Calvo and Bialystok, 2014).

Being Bilingual

If you know another language, you tend to have better executive function performance than if you know just one language (Calvo and Bialystok, 2014).

RISK FACTORS

Risk factors are those that make an individual more likely to have EF difficulties.

Genetics

As you read previously, ADHD, ASD, MDD, GAD, and cognitive disorders such as AD and Pick's Disease are highly heritable. Keep in mind that while individuals may have a genetic predisposition to develop a certain disorder, they may not actually end up manifesting any symptoms of the disorder. You can have the *genotype* for a disorder (the genes), but not the *phenotype* (expression of symptoms). For example, an individual may have a genetic predisposition to PTSD, but an environmental circumstance, trauma, causes the disorder to manifest.

Traumatic Brain Injury

TBI, particularly that which involves damage to the DLPFC, can cause executive dysfunction.

The Fascinating Case of Phineas Gage

In 1848, Phineas Gage was working as a railroad worker in Cavendish, Vermont. One day a tamping iron, a large metal bar used to pack explosive material into a hole, went through the frontal lobes of his brain due to an explosion. Gage survived - however, his personality and behavior changed drastically. He went from a hard-working man with an even temperament before the accident to a person who couldn't stick with plans, cursed frequently, started fights, and became an alcoholic (Twomey, 2010). This is what life looks like when your frontal lobes are no longer functional, leading to severe EF deficits, particularly in self-regulation and inhibition.

Low Neurotransmitter Levels

There are four main neurotransmitters or brain chemicals in humans that are related to EFs: dopamine, serotonin, norepinephrine, and gamma-aminobutryic acid (GABA). These neurotransmitters send signals from one neuron to another. When a person has EF difficulties, it may be due to the fact that neurotransmitter activity is low, particularly with regard to low activation of dopamine receptors in the prefrontal cortex. This, in turn, can lead to EF impairment, including difficulties with working memory (Shansky and Lipps, 2013).

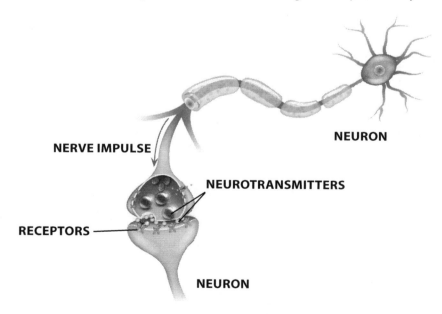

Medication and also non-medication treatments, such as exercise and mindfulness meditation, have been found to regulate neurotransmitter levels. You will learn about all these treatments later on in this workbook.

Changes in Hormone Levels

Women going through menopause may have increased difficulties with EF due to a decrease in estrogen production (Shanmugan and Epperson, 2014). Using hormone therapy during menopause can help improve executive function performance (Castonguay, Lussier, Bugaiska, Lord, and Bherer, 2015).

Chronic Stress

Experiencing chronic stress can lead to EF impairment, particularly with regard to cognitive flexibility and working memory (Shields, Sazma, and Yonelinas, 2016).

Exposure to Drugs in Utero

Children with fetal alcohol syndrome (FAS) have more impaired EF performance than children without FAS, and the rate of EF difficulties is directly proportional to the severity of FAS (Fuglestad et al., 2015). Children exposed to alcohol, nicotine, and methamphetamine in utero have more impaired EF performance compared to children who were not exposed in utero (Piper, Gray, Corbett, Birkett, and Raber, 2014). Children exposed to cocaine in utero also had more difficulties with EF tasks involving organizing, planning, and monitoring than non-exposed peers, with the more severely exposed children having greater difficulties with EF performance (Minnes et al., 2014).

Drug Use

Acute cannabis (marijuana) use leads to issues with attention and memory, while heavy use leads to difficulties with cognitive flexibility, perseveration, and difficulty with shifting and sustaining attention (Lundqvist, 2005). Methamphetamine use leads to impaired working memory, delayed recall, and slowed processing speed (Rusyniak, 2013). Users of 3,4-methylenedioxymethamphetamine (MDMA) experience a delay in verbal learning, recall, and distraction, as well as difficulty in paying attention to tasks and less efficiency in completing tasks (Wagner et al., 2013). Cocaine use leads to impairments in memory, reaction time, attention, learning, and cognitive flexibility (Lundqvist, 2005). One month of abstinence from cocaine was found to improve EF performance, particularly in working memory performance (Goncalves et al., 2014). Heroin use leads to difficulties with impulse control and selective processing (Yan et al., 2014). The more severe the drug use, the more severe the impact on EF (Lundqvist, 2005). Moreover, the effects of these drugs on EF can be long-lasting.

Poverty

Chronic poverty has been found to predict greater difficulties in EF performance among children (Raver, Blair, and Willoughby, 2013).

Abuse

Women addicted to crack cocaine and who experienced childhood neglect had poorer EF performance than those addicted to crack cocaine who did not have a history of childhood neglect (Viola et al., 2013). Moreover, among adolescents, physical abuse and neglect is correlated with issues in cognitive flexibility, even when the adolescents do not have a diagnosable *DSM* disorder (Spann et al., 2012).

YOUR CLIENT'S FIRST APPOINTMENT

A clinician is only as good as the information they have been given and their ability to interpret from that information. It is imperative that your client brings as much information as possible to their appointment. In this section, you will find forms to give your clients prior to their first appointment.

TIPS

Helping Clients Get a Good Family History

While members of your client's family would ideally attend his first appointment with you, it is not always possible to do so. The next best thing is for your client to ask family members relevant questions before his first appointment. However, before your client starts asking family members about their current and past mental health issues, it is important to let your client know that many families have difficulty talking about mental health issues in the family. The following recommendations may help your client have an easier time obtaining his family history:

- Have the client tell their family, "This information helps the doctor help me."

- Warn your client that he may find out things about their family that may be hard to hear. For example, your client may have thought her grandmother was overseas for six months, when in fact she was receiving inpatient treatment for bipolar disorder.

- If your client is adopted and it was a closed adoption, they may ask a judge to unseal their birth records, citing medical information as the cause. Judges are becoming increasingly understanding regarding the importance of an adoptee acquiring this information. Your client may also contact the adoption agency regarding procedures for getting in touch with their biological parents. Some adoption agencies also have family medical histories on file. It is important to note that the adoptive parents may not have received all the information in the file at the time of the adoption.

- Have your client ask the family if there is anyone in the family that just seemed "off." In a lot of families, individuals do not seek help from a mental health professional unless they are perceived as "really crazy." Therefore, there may be people in the family who have a diagnosable disorder and never sought help due to stigma of obtaining mental health services. This can be especially the case in a family where there are more severe disorders like schizophrenia – a family member with anxiety may not appear to be unhealthy to the family by relative comparison.

- Have your client ask about first-degree relatives (parents, siblings, children) and second-degree relatives (aunts, uncles, grandparents, and cousins). If a first-degree relative has an issue, it is much more likely that your client may have that issue.

- Your client also has the option of filling out a release of information form so you can talk with a family member directly about the family's medical history. Let the family member know from the outset that any information shared with you will also be shared with your client.

- Have your client fill out the family history form in this chapter. This is a helpful, organized way of keeping track of family history and what disorders to ask about.

Have your client ask about a family history of:

- ADHD
- Anxiety
- Depression
- Bipolar Disorder
- Psychiatric Hospitalizations
- "Nervous Breakdown" (now referred to as a psychotic break)

- Panic Disorder
- Suicide and Suicide Attempts
- Substance Abuse
- Seizures
- Sleep Disorders (sleep apnea, night terrors, sleepwalking)

The clinician worksheet, Family History Charts, on the next page can help you organize a client's family history. There's also one you can give to your client to fill out on their own.

After the Family History Charts you'll find a worksheet to give your clients before their first appointment. It lists the information you would like them to bring to the appointment. If you have a website, it is very helpful to include this list on a "forms" page for easy client access. You can also email this list to your clients after they schedule their first appointment. They can email it back, fax it to you, or bring it to their appointment. Inform your clients that electronic communication is never 100% secure.

Family History Chart

Directions: Use this chart to organize a client's family history.

Sz = Seizure; Sleep = Insomnia, sleep apnea, sleepwalking, night terrors. "Suicide" should be filled in if a family member has attempted or completed suicide. "Psychosis" includes a history of schizophrenia. To differentiate maternal and paternal family members, put an M or a P in the corresponding box.

	ADHD	Anx	Dep	Bipolar	SUD	Psychosis	Suicide	ASD	Sz	Sleep
Mother										
Father										
Sibling										
Sibling										
Child										
Child										
Aunt										
Uncle										
Aunt										
Uncle										
Cousin										
Cousin										
Grandmother										
Grandfather										

Notes

_____

_____

_____

_____

_____

_____

_____

_____

Family History Chart

	ADHD	Depression	Anxiety	Bipolar	Drug Abuse
Mother					
Father					
Sibling					
Sibling					
Sibling					
Child					
Child					
Child					
Aunt					
Aunt					
Uncle					
Uncle					
Cousin					
Cousin					
Cousin					
Cousin					

	Autism	Suicide	OCD	Tics	Sleep Issues
Mother					
Father					
Sibling					
Sibling					
Sibling					
Child					
Child					
Child					
Aunt					
Aunt					
Uncle					
Uncle					
Cousin					
Cousin					
Cousin					
Cousin					

What You Should Bring to Your First Appointment

In order to best help you, please bring any of the following documents to your first appointment. You can also fax this paperwork to me at _____ or email it to me at _____. Please be aware that electronic communication is never 100% secure.

If you need copies of your medical records, please contact me to sign a release form so I can obtain copies for you. It is recommended that I receive copies directly from the doctor's office. If you request and pick up your own records, you may have to pay for the copies.

- Documentation
    - Report cards
    - Work performance reports
    - Medical records
    - Testing records
    - Letters from family and friends discussing what behaviors they have noticed in you, from childhood forward

- A list of medications you are taking
    - Name of medication
    - Dose of medication
    - When you take the medication
    - List of side effects or benefits for each medication

- Family history notes
    - Who in the family has had:
        - Attention deficit hyperactivity disorder
        - Depression
        - Anxiety
        - Bipolar disorder
        - Substance abuse or dependence
        - Psychosis
        - Attempted or completed suicide
        - Seizures
        - Autism spectrum disorder
        - Sleep disorders, like sleep apnea and sleepwalking
    - Please note if your family member has received treatment for a disorder, what the treatment was, and if it was successful or unsuccessful.

Questions to Answer Before
Your First Appointment

To help your therapist, answer and elaborate on the following questions before your first appointment, and bring this paper with you:

1. Are you continually arguing with others, like your partner/spouse, family members, friends and coworkers?

_____

_____

_____

_____

_____

2. Are you in trouble at work because you haven't completed projects or assignments?

_____

_____

_____

_____

_____

3. Are you in debt because of impulsive spending?

_____

_____

_____

_____

_____

4. Have you had a head injury? If so, when and what happened?

_____

_____

_____

_____

_____

5. Do you avoid socializing because you are concerned you'll interrupt others or say the wrong thing?

_____

_____

_____

_____

6. Do you get late fees on bills because you can't remember to pay them on time?

_____

_____

_____

_____

7. Do you feel like you've had a lifetime of not working to your potential?

_____

_____

_____

_____

8. Has your ability to focus and pay attention decreased as you've gotten older, or has it always been there at the same level?

_____

_____

_____

_____

9. What are your top three concerns at this time?

_____

_____

_____

_____

Getting a Good Life
History Timeline

When you are meeting your client for an initial evaluation, keep in mind that he may have difficulties with time management. This leads to difficulties estimating time and knowing when events happened – and that is essential information to obtain. When you are asking about certain life events, use "benchmarks" or holidays to determine what happened when. To obtain benchmarks, ask your client about:

• A significant event that happened this week
• A significant event that happened this month
• A significant event that happened this year
• A significant event in the past five years

For example, when you ask your client when they graduated, they may give an answer that is not entirely correct – not on purpose, but because their brain has difficulty with dates and time estimation.

Instead, ask your client, "Did you graduate after your Caribbean cruise and before your surprise 30th birthday party?"

You can narrow it down even further by relating the passing of time to holidays. For example, "Did you graduate between Valentine's Day and St. Patrick's Day?" Getting a timeline by using benchmarks can result in a more accurate picture of your client's life events. With a signed release, you can also verify these dates with a family member.

December						
SUNDAY	MONDAY	TUESDAY	WEDNESDAY	THURSDAY	FRIDAY	SATURDAY
					1	2
3	4	5	6	7	8	9
10	11	12	13	14	15	16
17	18	19	20	21	22	23
24	25	26	27	28	29	30
31						

Intake Form

When meeting with a client, use the following form to keep your information organized:

Name_____   Date of Intake_____

Date of Birth _____   Born in _____   Born in _____

CLIENT'S MAIN CONCERN

_____

_____

_____

HISTORY OF CURRENT ISSUE

_____

_____

_____

PAST PSYCHIATRIC HISTORY

_____

_____

_____

FAMILY HISTORY *(Use in conjunction with the family history chart)*

Siblings _____

Parents _____

Parents' Level of Education and Occupations

_____

_____

PARENTS: *Married, Divorced, or Never Married?* _____

If no longer together, when did they separate, divorce, or split up? _____

DEVELOPMENTAL HISTORY

Mother's pregnancy, labor and delivery

_____

_____

Did the mother smoke, drink, or use drugs during her pregnancy?_____

Was the client born at term? _____ Weight at birth _____

When did mother and baby leave the hospital? _____

MILESTONES

Crawled _____ Walked _____ Said First Word _____

Spoke in Sentences _____ Was Toilet Trained _____

Rode a Bicycle Without Training Wheels _____

EDUCATIONAL HISTORY

Elementary school

_____

Middle school

_____

High school

_____

College

_____

Post college

_____

OCCUPATIONAL HISTORY

Job _____ Dates Employed_____ Why client left _____

Job _____ Dates Employed_____ Why client left _____

Job _____ Dates Employed_____ Why client left _____

MEDICAL HISTORY

Surgeries, hospitalizations

_____

_____

Current prescriptions

_____

_____

Past prescriptions

_____

_____

History of substance abuse

_____

_____

Diagnostic impressions

_____

_____

_____

_____

PLAN

_____

_____

_____

_____

_____

_____

ASSESSING EF DIFFICULTIES

How do you know if your client has difficulties with EFs? There are two ways to assess executive function difficulties in a clinical setting. At the end of this workbook, in Appendix A, you will find a list of EF tests. You will also learn what assessments might be available outside of your office.

Keep in mind that EF performance can differ based on:

- Medication taken
- Amount of sleep
- Nature of test
- Already existing skill set

Two methods to assess EF difficulties are rating scales and performance tests. At this point, genetic testing and brain scans cannot be used to diagnose EF difficulties or specific disorders.

Executive Function Rating Scales

These scales are non-invasive and easily accessible. You can also score the results right in your office. Examples of EF ratings scales include:

Frontal Systems Behavior Scale (FrSBe)

The FrSBe measures three issues: apathy, disinhibition, and executive dysfunction. It looks at both a client's past behavior and current behavior. It consists of 46 items and is completed by the client and a family member. It is scored by the clinician. The qualification level is a "B," meaning that in order to administer this scale, you must have a graduate degree in psychology or counseling from an accredited university, and have specific training in psychometrics. It takes roughly 10 minutes to administer, and up to 15 minutes to score.

Behavior Rating Inventory of Executive Function – Adult Version (BRIEF-A)

The BRIEF-A is completed by the client and a family member. It is scored by the clinician or by computer. It takes approximately 20 minutes to complete and 20 minutes to score. This scale has a "B" qualification level. Categories scored on the BRIEF-A include emotional control, planning/organization, and working memory, among others.

Barkley Deficits in Executive Functioning Scale (BDEFS for Adults)

The BDEFS is completed by the client and a family member. There are long form and short form versions. The long form version takes about 15-20 minutes to complete, while the short form version takes about 5 minutes to complete. The scales and scoring sheets can be reproduced an unlimited amount of times with the purchase of the test. The BDEFS looks at issues of time management, organization, motivation, emotion regulation, and problem-solving.

Executive Function Performance Tests

Some performance tests for executive function assessment are administered by a clinician, while others are completed by the client on a computer. Some of these tests are referred to as "go/no-go." This means that the client is asked to click with the mouse or hit the space bar when they see a particular stimulus, and to refrain from reacting when a different stimulus or no stimulus is on the screen.

Continuous Performance Test (CPT) 3™

The CPT is a go/no-go computer-based test that measures the variables of inattentiveness, impulsivity, sustained attention, and vigilance. The test also measures detectability, (the ability to differentiate between particular stimuli,) and omissions (erroneously not reacting to a particular stimulus).

Tower of London/Tower of Hanoi

The TOL (TOH) is either administered by the clinician or taken on a computer. In the in-person version, the clinician and the client each have a rectangular board with three pegs – short, medium, and tall. There are also three beads on each board – red, green, and blue. For two practice problems and 10 scored problems, the clinician presents the bead pattern the client should achieve on their board. The amount of moves required to solve the bead pattern increases with each problem. The TOL measures variables such as rule violations, total move scores, and total initiation time.

Tests of Variables of Attention (TOVA®)

The TOVA® is a 21-minute go/no-go computer-based test that measures response to a visual or an auditory stimulus. In the visual portion, the client tries to differentiate a specific shape from another shape when they pop up on the screen. The auditory part of the test has the client differentiate a specific tone from another tone. The test variables include response time, commission errors, and omission errors.

Quotient Test

The Quotient Test is also a computer-based go/no-go test. In addition to having stimuli on the screen, the client also wears motion sensors on their head, arms, and legs. While responding to stimuli on the screen, the Quotient Test measures how much the client is moving while taking the test. The results of the Quotient Test provide measures of the go/no-go task, plus a rendering of the amount of motor activity a client exhibited during the test.

Wisconsin Card Sorting Test (WCST)

The WCST is administered by a clinician or taken on a computer. Cards with various patterns of shapes are shown to the client. The client is told to match the cards. but is not told the rules of what is considered a match. However, as the client proceeds through the tasks, the clinician states whether a match is connect or incorrect. The test takes up to 20 minutes to administer. Variables measured include categories achieved and perseverative errors. The WCST is known as a set-shifting task. This means the test measures a client's cognitive flexibility, especially when the matching "rules" change often.

The Stroop Color-Word Test

The Stroop gauges the brain's ability to regulate interference, or competing stimuli. In the Stroop, the client is presented with a list of words written in different colors, but the color of the word is different than what the word represents. For example, "green" is written in blue, "yellow" is written in red, and so on. The client is asked to say the *color* of the word, not the word itself. If a person has executive dysfunction, it is more difficult to separate out the color of the word. The brain has a tendency to say the actual word as written.

Should My Client Stop Their Medication Before EF Testing?

Generally, it is best to get an idea of how a client functions in their day-to-day life. If a client is taking stimulant medication, then it has already been integrated into their regular activities and day-to-day functioning. If you would like a client to refrain from taking medication for the test, you must get this cleared with their prescribing physician first.

As you learned earlier, there is no single test to fully assess executive functions. The best approach is to combine testing along with:

- Clinical interview
- Additional rating scales and testing
- Review of collateral data
  - Doctor's notes
  - School reports
  - Work performance reviews

CHAPTER 3 Medication & Supplements

Medication is usually the first-line or primary treatment for disorders involving executive dysfunction, including ADHD (Antshel et al., 2011). Stimulants and antidepressants are the most commonly prescribed medications for these issues. You may have also seen clients take supplements such as Omega 3-6-9 to help treat executive function EF difficulties. In this chapter, you will learn about the benefits and side effects of medication for executive dysfunction and also some "buyer beware" issues with supplements. You will also see how Omega 3-6-9 has been helping somewhat with EF performance.

MEDICATION

Medications, particularly stimulant medication, may improve executive function performance, particularly when a client has ADHD. When a client is taking stimulant medication, there is a biological change in how the brain takes in, processes, and stores information. If you have a client off medication one week and on medication the next, you may see quite a difference. When stimulant medication is "on board," your client may have better eye contact, may be able to accurately repeat back to you what you have discussed, and may even sit still during the session. Off medication, your client may not seem to be not fully connecting with you, and they may ask you to repeat things that you have said. They also may appear to be more restless and may even ask you if the appointment is over yet.

Studies have found that psychotropic medications and behavioral treatments used in conjunction can enhance the effectiveness of each treatment (Pelham et al., 2014; Jensen, 2009). Oftentimes, medication is recommended along with another form of treatment, such as counseling (Antshel and Barkley, 2008). In essence, "pills" may be needed in order to learn the "skills" taught in counseling sessions.

STIMULANT MEDICATIONS

Stimulant medications have been available by prescription in the U.S. since 1937 (Purushothaman, 2013). Therefore, there is quite a bit of longitudinal data available about this type of medication. Studies have not found any evidence of permanent brain "rewiring," stunted height, or malnutrition associated with the use of stimulant medication with the exception of an already existing cardiac issue. Heart issues have also not been found to be an issue with stimulant medication (Cooper et al., 2011; Schelleman et al., 2011). Of course, your client should let any of their doctors know if there is a personal or family history of cardiac issues in the family (Warren et al., 2009).

With regard to concerns that clients may become "addicted" to stimulant medications, studies have found stimulant medications have either have no effect, or even *reduce* an individual's chances of addiction. Stimulant medication has also been found to decrease the chances of relapse in recovering addicts (Konstenius, Jayaram-Lindström, Guterstam, Beck, Philips, and Franck, 2014; Chang et al., 2013; Molina et al., 2013; Biederman et al., 2008; Biederman, 2003; Wilens et al., 2004). Stimulants work by increasing dopamine and norepinephrine activation in the dorsolateral prefrontal cortex (DLPFC). Side effects include dry mouth, difficulty sleeping, and appetite suppression.

Usually extended-release stimulants are prescribed once a day. If your client has longer work hours or has an activity after work, the doctor may prescribe an immediate-release stimulant to take before the extended-release stimulant wears off.

TIPS

Stimulant Medications

Stimulant Medications include:

- Extended-release (half-life or effectiveness is 8 to 12 hours)
    - Concerta (extended-release methylphenidate)
    - Vyvanse (lisdexamfetamine)
    - Daytrana (methylphenidate transdermal)
    - Focalin XR (dexmethylphenidate extended-release)
    - Adderall XR (extended-release dextroamphetamine of mixed salts)
    - Dexedrine spansule (dextroamphetamine)

- Immediate-release (half-life or effectiveness is 3 to 4 hours)
    - Ritalin (methylphenidate)
    - Focalin (dexmethylphenidate)
    - Dexedrine (dextroamphetamine)

Schedule II Medications

Stimulant medications are classified as "Schedule II" medications by the U.S. Drug Enforcement Agency (DEA). This means that stimulant medications are "controlled substances," medications which the DEA has classified as having a high potential for abuse. However, stimulant medications are prescribed at a fairly low dosage. As you read earlier, studies have found taking stimulant medication does not increase, and may even decrease, the chances of substance abuse in people with ADHD.

Because of this Schedule II designation, however, your client cannot have his stimulant prescription called into the pharmacy. They must pick up the prescription from their doctor or have the prescription mailed to them. In some states physicians must send stimulant prescriptions electronically to the pharmacy. If you are in a state that requires a paper prescription for stimulants, this means that your client will need extra time to get a new prescription before they run out of their current medication. It is recommended that either the doctor's office calls to remind your client to get a new prescription or you help your client schedule in their calendar when they need to contact their doctor for a new prescription.

Remind your client that if they are taking a Schedule II stimulant, he will test positive for amphetamines on a drug test. They must bring their medication bottle with them if they are getting drug tested for a job. If your client is an athlete, he will need to show the team doctor the medication bottle as soon as possible.

The following client handouts can be given to your clients to help them understand their medications better:

- Stimulant shortage information
- Your rights at the pharmacy
- Taking your medication
- Information on medication
- Medication information sheet for your doctor

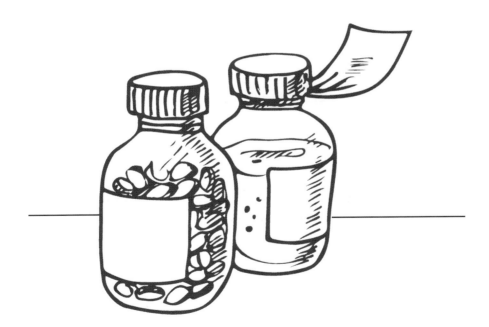

Stimulant Shortage Information

There is currently a stimulant shortage in the U.S. The Food and Drug Administration (FDA) and the Drug Enforcement Agency (DEA) are currently in disagreement about ending this shortage due to quotas that the DEA sets on the quantity of controlled substances that can be manufactured.

As a result, many pharmacies have stimulant medications on backorder. You may find that one month your local pharmacy has your medication, but the next month you have to go from one pharmacy to another to find one that has your medication in stock.

Until this shortage is resolved, if you are unable to get your stimulant medication prescription filled at your local pharmacy, here are some options:

1. Ask the pharmacist if the medication is available at another location.
   Some pharmacists will give you this information; some will not.

2. Call other pharmacies in the area to see if the medication is in stock.

3. Contact the medication manufacturer to see where a pharmacy may have it in stock.

4. Ask your prescriber about the availability of other stimulant medications for ADHD.

5. Report a medication shortage to the FDA at drugshortages@fda.hhs.gov.
   Be aware that you will not get a personalized response.

Your Rights at the Pharmacy

When you go to the pharmacy, it is important to know what you can expect and what you should not tolerate. The following is a list of the pharmacist's/pharmacy's rights and your rights as a consumer.

It is within the pharmacist's/pharmacy's legal rights to:

1. Refuse to fill a prescription.

2. Refuse to stock a medication.

3. Ask you for what condition you are taking the medication.

4. Ask you what other medical conditions you may have.

5. Tell you about interactions with other medications you might be taking.

6. Tell you about equivalent (same) medications.

You also have rights in a pharmacy. You have the right to:

1. Be treated respectfully.

2. Ask for the pharmacist. There should always be a pharmacist on site.

3. Ask the pharmacist questions about your medication.

4. Ask why a prescription is not being filled.

5. Speak to the pharmacist in a private, confidential setting.

6. Be told when the medication is available for pickup.

A pharmacist is not allowed to make personal value judgments about you or your medication. An example of a personal value judgment would be if the pharmacist said, "I don't think you should take that medication," without giving you a reasonable medical explanation. If you feel your rights have been violated at a pharmacy, contact the corporate office, and get your prescriptions filled at another pharmacy.

How Stimulant Medication Impacts EFs

Stimulant medication can significantly improve executive functioning. Several studies have been conducted looking at how stimulant medication changes the manner in which neurons in the brain fire. In particular, when an individual is not taking stimulant medication, there are areas of the brain that fire when they shouldn't, and areas that aren't firing when they should. When study subjects are taking stimulant medication, functional magnetic resonance imaging (fMRI) has found more activation in the dorsolateral prefrontal cortex and the parietal cortex during an executive function task than when they were not taking medication and compared to a control group (Bush et al., 2008). Another study found that stimulant medication, when added to behavioral interventions, helped improve working memory (Strand et al., 2012).

Because stimulant medication makes such an impact on executive functioning, it is important when conducting a study on EF treatments that subjects are all either on medication or off medication. Otherwise, the researchers are introducing a *confounding variable* into the study. This means that it is unclear if the treatment was effective on its own, or if subjects responded better to the treatment because they were taking medication.

What does this mean for you in practice? As you read earlier in this chapter, it means that a brain characterized by executive dysfunction is behaving in a fundamentally different way when your client is taking medication. If your client is on medication one week and off it the next, you may need to provide more structure, write instructions down, add more novelty to the session, and have your client repeat things back to you.

Stimulant Medications and Driving

When you drive, you are engaging EFs that involve time management, planning, emotion regulation, and forethought. One study found that young adults with ADHD taking stimulant medication had significantly improved driving performance on a simulator compared to a group that was taking a placebo. In addition, 80% of subjects who were taking stimulant medications reduced their ADHD rating scale scores by at least 30% (Kay et al., 2009). That is quite a large jump. If a client is not taking stimulant medication, they run the risk of having increased collisions and hazard-response time on a driving simulator compared to when they are on their medication (Trick and Toxopeus, 2013). In addition, a study found that individuals with ADHD who texted or talked on their cell phone while driving in a simulator had significantly greater driving impairment than their non-ADHD counterparts who engaged in the same activities (Kingery, Garner, Antonini, Tamm, and Epstein, 2015). There are apps that will prohibit your client from texting while the phone senses driving movement. For more information, see the Resources section at the end of this workbook.

Stimulant Medication and Compliance

Given that a person with EF difficulties may have issues with organization, planning, and forethought, they can tend to skip doses or double-dose themselves, not realizing they had already taken their medication. Studies have found that skipping doses or taking a "drug holiday" tends to decrease individuals' overall ability to cope with their day-to-day life and puts added strain on their relationships. Your client continues to have EF difficulties when they are not at work or school. Next you will find a handout for your client to help improve medication compliance.

Taking Your Medication

When you have issues with executive functions, you may be more likely to skip a dose or double-dose yourself. Here are ways to make sure you take your medication on a regular basis:

MEDICATION TIPS

- Buy four weekly pill containers, or a one-month container. Set a notification on your calendar to refill your pill container every month on the 1st.

- Double-check to make sure you are taking pills from the right day of the week of your container.

- Set timers on your phone to notify you when it is time to take your pill.

- If you take your pills first thing in the morning, leave your pill container next to your breakfast plate or on your nightstand.

- Because federal law prohibits stimulant medication from being called into a pharmacy, make sure you call your doctor's office when you have two weeks of stimulant medication left in order to give yourself a little buffer time.

- If you have drug testing at your place of employment, you must bring your medication bottle with you. If you take stimulant medication, you will test positive for amphetamines.

- If you are an athlete, let your team doctor know as soon as possible that you are taking medication, and bring the bottle with you.

- If you need to bring a medication bottle to work or to school, ask the pharmacist to put your medication in two separate labeled bottles.

- If you live with roommates, keep your medication in a locked safety box, bolted to your wall. Do not keep it in your medicine cabinet – addicts will tell you that's the first place they look for medication.

- Never give out your medication for any reason. First, it's illegal. Second, if a person dies as a result of taking your medication, you may be convicted of involuntary manslaughter.

Stimulant Medication and Diversion

You may have seen stories on the media and also heard your clients talking about the abuse of stimulant medication. One study of over 9,000 college students found that the rate of stimulant abuse on campus by those not prescribed the medication was 8.1% (McCabe, Teter, and Boyd, 2006). The number of students who abused stimulants was found to exceed the number of students diagnosed with ADHD who used stimulants as prescribed. Also, students who had been taking their prescribed stimulant medication since elementary school did not have an increased risk of illicit stimulant prescription use (McCabe, Teter, and Boyd, 2006).

Sometimes medication can be stolen from a person who is appropriately prescribed it for ADHD. For this reason, the warning of "keep your medication in a locked bolted safe" was added to the medication tip worksheet above.

It used to be believed that if you had ADHD, your diagnosis would be verified if stimulant medication improved your symptoms. However, stimulant medication helps anyone focus better. However, as you learned earlier in the chapter, stimulants work by activating dopamine in your brain. If you have a normal dopamine level, taking stimulants can kick your dopamine level up too high – resulting in auditory hallucination and formication (the sensation of bugs crawling on your skin).

Stimulant Medications and Their Impact on Overall Functioning

Stimulant medications have been found to increase clients' quality of life, particularly among those with ADHD (Surman et al., 2013; Coghill, 2010). Stimulant medication increases the rate of employment in ADHD adults, and the earlier a client starts on medication, the more of a chance they have of being employed (Gjervan et al., 2012; Pietras et al., 2003). Stimulant medication also decreases impulsive high-risk financial choices (Halmey et al., 2009).

NONSTIMULANT MEDICATION

In addition to stimulant medication, antidepressants and other nonstimulant medications can be prescribed for the treatment of ADHD. Unlike stimulant medication, non-stimulant medication is not labeled by the FDA as having an addictive potential and therefore can be called into the pharmacy. However, studies have found that non-stimulant medications may not be as effective as stimulant medications in one particular disorder characterized by executive dysfunction: ADHD (Faraone and Glatt, 2010). Although not as effective in treating EF deficits, non-stimulants may be prescribed instead of stimulants for the following reasons:

- When a person would just prefer not to take stimulant medication
- If a person has unwanted side effects to stimulant medication
- If a person has a history of drug abuse

Many times, stimulant medications and non-stimulant medications are prescribed together, and the FDA has given its approval for this (Treuer et al., 2013). When taking non-stimulant medications, it is very important that your client consults with his doctor before discontinuing the medication. Abrupt discontinuation of non-stimulant medications can cause unwanted reactions. This is why it is always important that you, as a clinician, have open communication with prescribers.

Strattera (atomoxetine)

In 2002, Strattera was the first non-stimulant approved by the FDA for the treatment of ADHD. It is an antidepressant that is in a class of medications called selective norepinephrine reuptake inhibitors (sNRIs). This means that the medication allows more norepinephrine (a neurotransmitter) to linger in the synapse, which is the space between neurons. Similar to other antidepressants, it may take several weeks for Strattera to become effective.

Strattera has been found to significantly decrease the severity of hyperactive and inattentive symptoms in adults with ADHD compared to a placebo (Adler et al., 2014; Schwartz and Correll, 2014; Newcorn, Kratochvil, and Allen, 2008). However, one study found that 40% of participants still had significant ADHD symptoms (Schwartz and Correll, 2014). In another study, Strattera was found to significantly improve executive function performance in adults with ADHD versus those who took a placebo pill (Brown et al., 2011). Strattera can be helpful for individuals who have not had success with stimulant medication or for those who have depression and anxiety in addition to ADHD (Hammerness et al., 2009; Vaughan, Fegert, and Kratochvil, 2009). The most common side effects of Strattera include upset stomach, dry mouth, dizziness, and decreased appetite.

How Strattera Works

As you learned earlier in the section on stimulant medication, there are neurons that send information and neurons that receive information. The space between a sending and receiving neuron is called the *synapse*. You need to have enough neurotransmitters hanging out in the synapse and for a long enough period of time for information to flow from the sending neuron to the receiving neuron. In ADHD, the neurotransmitters can be reabsorbed too quickly by the sending neuron. Strattera stops the neurotransmitter norepinephrine from being reabsorbed into the sending neuron too quickly.

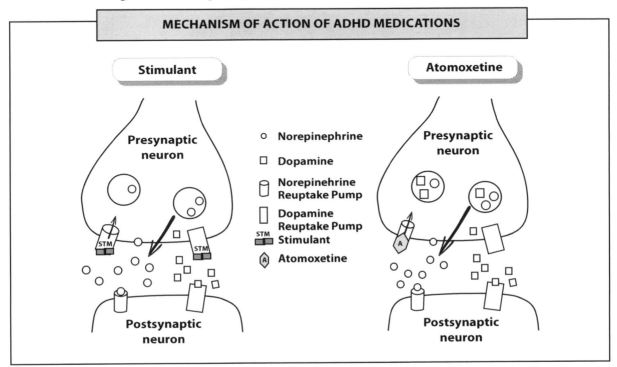

Intuniv (guanfacine extended-release)

In 2009, Intuniv was FDA-approved for the treatment of ADHD. Intuniv is a selective α_{2A} receptor agonist, which interacts with receptors in the prefrontal cortex of the brain. Intuniv was originally a medication that the FDA approved for the treatment of high blood pressure. While the medication's mechanism action of high blood pressure is known, researchers don't know exactly how Intuniv works in the frontal lobe to help decrease impulsivity and improve focus. In one study, Intuniv was found to significantly reduce hyperactivity, impulsivity, and inattentiveness compared to a placebo (Biederman, Melmed, and Patel, 2008). In another study, Intuniv was found to be significantly more effective at reducing ADHD symptoms than Strattera (Sikirica et al., 2013). Intuniv side effects include low blood pressure, dry mouth, and drowsiness (Cruz, 2010). In addition, you may have to take Intuniv for up to two weeks or more before you see benefits.

Kapvay (clonidine hydrochloride)

In 2010, Kapvay was FDA-approved for the treatment of ADHD (Thomas, 2013). It is known as a centrally-acting α_2 adrenergic agonist and works in the prefrontal cortex of the brain. Like Intuniv, the FDA initially approved the immediate-release version of Kapvay for the treatment of high blood pressure. Like Intuniv, Kapvay's mechanism of action is known for treating high blood pressure, but it is not known exactly how it works in the frontal lobe. In some studies, Kapvay has been found to significantly reduce ADHD symptoms versus placebo (Jain et al., 2011). It has also been found to help significantly reduce ADHD symptoms in subjects who were taking stimulant medication at the same time (Kollins et al., 2011). Side effects of Kapvay include drowsiness, dizziness, fatigue, and low blood pressure (Ming, Mulvey, Mohanty, and Patel, 2011). As with other non-stimulant medications, have your client speak with his doctor if you want to discontinue the medication. Suddenly stopping Kapvay can cause withdrawal symptoms, such as increased blood pressure, headache, and feeling lightheaded.

Information on Medication

HOW LONG DO I NEED TO TAKE THIS MEDICATION?

I wish there was a way to take a crystal ball and see. Some people find that they benefit so much from medication that they take it on a long-term basis. Others take the medication, feel that they have learned skills to cope with their issues, and then stop the medication. It really depends on the individual.

HOW MUCH WILL THIS MEDICATION COST?

Your medication cost can differ based on your health insurance coverage and whether you are taking generic or brand name medication. If you call your insurance company to see if they cover your medication, it is important to get that information in writing – email or regular mail. Insurance companies are not required to honor statements made over the phone. If you are unable to afford your medication, some pharmaceutical companies have programs where you can receive certain medications at a lower cost if you provide proof of hardship.

HOW WILL I KNOW IF I HAVE A SIDE EFFECT?

If you are ever not feeling like yourself, give your doctor a call. Your doctor's name

is _____ and their phone number is _____.

Doctors want you to call if there is an issue with your medication. They would much rather find out now so a change can be made.

Medication Information Sheet for Your Doctor

Sometimes it can be difficult to remember what medication you are taking and any side effects you may be having. Take this sheet with you to your next doctor's appointment so you can make sure to remember what you need to talk about.

Name_____   Date_____

Why I am here today:

The good things I have noticed since my last appointment:

The not-so-good things I have noticed since my last appointment (including side effects):

The way things are going is (circle one)   **better   the same   worse**   since my last appointment.

My current medications:

Name	Dosage	When I take it
1.		
2.		
3.		
4.		
5.		
6.		

Medications I am allergic to:

Other doctors or counselors I have met with since my last appointment:

SUPPLEMENTS

In this section you will learn about supplements – quality control issues, side effects, and whether a person with executive dysfunction even really needs to take them. You will also learn how you or your client can find a good quality company if you want to go the supplement route. Supplements (also referred to as "nutraceuticals," to sound similar to "pharmaceuticals") are capsules, tablets, powders, and other forms that contain vitamins, minerals or "natural" ingredients. So-called "natural" ingredients include products from plants, like St. John's wort, valerian root, and kava. However, the term "natural" is not regulated by any U.S. governmental agency. In this section, you will also learn the importance of knowing exactly what your client is taking, including supplements. Supplements can impact the central nervous system (CNS) and change how your body absorbs medication. It is essential that we keep open communication with prescribers so that we are all "on the same page." Later in this section, you will find a chart for recording all of your client's prescriptions and supplements. Ask your client to sign releases for their prescribers, and share information regarding these medications and supplements with them.

Supplements have become quite popular, making $32.5 billion dollars in 2012, an increase of 7.5% in just one year (Garcia-Cazarin, Wambogo, Regan, and Davis, 2014).

SUPPLEMENTS AND QUALITY CONTROL ISSUES

While they may be popular, there are questions about supplement quality. Following a 1994 federal act called the Dietary Supplement Health and Education Act (DSHEA), supplements no longer need to meet the same FDA strict approval process that pharmaceutical drugs do. According to the DSHEA, supplements are not categorized as pharmaceutical drugs (i.e., medications) (Buscemi et al., 2004). According to the FDA, dietary supplements are not intended to treat, diagnose, cure, or alleviate the effects of diseases.

The DSHEA allows supplement companies to market and put their products on the shelves of grocery stores and pharmacies without needing any FDA approval. The FDA does eventually step in when complaints have been made about a particular dietary supplement.

The FDA has what are called "Good Manufacturing Practices" (GMPs) that it requires pharmaceutical or pharmaceutical device manufacturers to follow. If the FDA finds that a pharmaceutical or pharmaceutical device manufacturer has violated any of the GMPs, they are shut down almost immediately. In the case of supplements, the FDA investigates if a certain amount of people have complained or if there have been injuries or deaths from a supplement. It's a much different standard of safety.

The issue of quality of supplements is an important one. Some studies have found that the concentration of a supplement can vary greatly from product to product (Curtis and Gaylord, 2005). This means that in one supplement bottle you may get 25mg in each capsule, while another bottle with the same product and manufacturer might give you a different dosage. Some studies have found that supplement dosage can even vary from capsule to capsule in one bottle, and the bottle may not contain what the label on the bottle says it does (Zhao, Zhang, Wei, Fan, Sun, and Bai, 2014; Curtis and Gaylord, 2005).

Rules for Supplements

"Supplements," according to the Dietary Supplement Health and Education Act (DSHEA), include vitamins, minerals, herbal preparations, fiber, amino acid, and Omega supplements. According to the DSHEA, in order for a "dietary supplement" to be sold to the general public, it has to meet the following criteria:

- It is intended to be added to a diet, not used as a meal replacement

- It must contain a vitamin, herb, amino acid or any combination of those

- It has labeling stating it is a dietary supplement

In addition, supplement bottles must state:

- "Dietary supplement" or the name of the product, such as "Ginkgo supplement"

- The number of capsules/pills in the bottle

- A nutrition label, including the serving size and percent of daily value met by each ingredient

- If the supplement is a blend, the amount of each ingredient in the blend plus a list of the ingredients, starting from most prevalent to least prevalent

- The part of the plant used (leaves, roots, bark)

- The name and location of the manufacturer

- A complete list of ingredients by their common names

- Safety information, including side effects that may result from taking the supplement

- The disclaimer, "This statement has not been evaluated by the Food and Drug Administration. This product is not intended to diagnose, treat, cure, or prevent any disease" if the product claims to improve health or wellbeing

Keep in mind that in the U.S., there is no government regulation on the word "natural." That means that any product (or food) be labeled "natural."

Finding a Supplement with Good Quality Control

Due to reduced government control over supplements, it is very important that if clients want to go this route, they find a supplement manufacturer that practices good quality assurance, or high standards in manufacturing. Supplement labeling can be tricky, so here are some ways to help your clients determine if they should buy a certain supplement.

Your client may see "Follows FDA's Good Manufacturing Practices" printed on supplement bottles (Frankos et al., 2010). As you learned earlier in this chapter, the FDA's Good Manufacturing Practices (GMPs) are a set of rules that pharmaceutical and pharmaceutical device manufacturers must follow. However, if a supplement label states a product or manufacturer follows the FDA's GMPs it does not mean the FDA checks to make sure they are following those practices.

When you are looking up quality control data for a supplement manufacturer, you want the answers to at least these four questions:

1. Is the manufacturing facility clean and well maintained?

2. Is the supplement's ingredient list accurate? (Is there anything in the capsule/tablet that isn't listed on the ingredients label?)

3. Is there uniform dosing? (Does each pill/capsule in a bottle have the same milligrams?)

4. Is the quality control check done randomly (without prior notice) and performed by an independent company (not paid by the manufacturer)?

You can find a company's quality control data on their website, in their investor's shareholder report, or you can call the company for their quality control information. ConsumerLab.com conducts analysis of supplements and can be accessed for a yearly fee. Check a company's quality control data on a regular basis, as companies can change owners and manufacturing locations often.

To find out more about supplements and quality control data, please see the Resources section at the end of this workbook.

Keeping Open Communication with Prescribers

Supplements can impact your client's central nervous system (CNS). They can also change how the body absorbs medication. It's very important that you find out anything your client is taking – prescribed medication, herbal supplements, vitamins, minerals, and powders. Ask your clients to bring everything they are taking in a bag. Use the following chart to help you keep track of what your clients are taking:

Name of Substance	Mg/mcg	Dosing	Benefits	Side Effects	Other

Herbal Supplements

Double-blind placebo-controlled studies have found that none of the following herbal supplements help treat executive dysfunction, nor the disorders associated with them (Hurt, Arnold, and Lofthouse, 2011; Sawni, 2008):

- o Valerian root
- o Kava
- o St. John's wort
- o Ginkgo biloba
- o Ginseng

If your client is taking an herbal supplement, it is very important that his doctors are informed of the product and frequency of ingestion. The supplements listed above can impact the CNS and result in side effects such as dizziness, drowsiness, respiratory distress, mania, and ataxia. These supplements can also affect the way your client's body absorbs and uses medication (Mitra et al., 2010; Izzo & Ernst, 2009; Foti et al., 2007). St. John's wort, ginkgo biloba, and ginseng can act as anticoagulants (blood thinners), and kava can cause liver damage or failure.

Melatonin

Melatonin is a hormone the brain releases when it is getting ready to go to sleep. Melatonin is also found in some plants, including fruit. As you will read in Chapter 7, sleep disorders are a big issue for people with executive dysfunction. Some individuals with executive dysfunction, such as those with ADHD, release melatonin too late, which leads to initial insomnia (Biljenga et al., 2013; Snitselaar and Smits, 2014; Van Veen et al., 2010). Melatonin supplements have been touted as a way to get better sleep. It is usually taken in tablet, liquid, capsule, or soft gel form. Clients may tell you all sorts of different ways they dose themselves with melatonin, which is a sign that a supplement is not effective. When a pharmaceutical drug has gone through the strict FDA testing process, it has dosage parameters. In addition to executive dysfunction, melatonin has been tested in studies on depression, sleep disorders, and sexual dysfunction. Some studies that have been conducted on melatonin supplements among individuals with ADHD have shown that it might help with insomnia, but not with ADHD symptoms (Miner, 2012).

There is just not enough research on melatonin supplements to establish them as an effective treatment for ADHD or other disorders characterized by executive function deficits (Holvoet and Gabriëls, 2013). However, in the case of *pharmaceutical-grade* melatonin (regulated by the FDA), it has been found to be effective in combination with sleep hygiene intervention in treating initial insomnia in children with ADHD (Weiss, Wasdell, Bomben, Rea, and Freeman, 2006).

Side effects of melatonin supplements include nausea, sluggishness, drowsiness, irritability, and hypothermia (Bauer, 2011). If your client has an autoimmune disorder such as lupus, multiple sclerosis, or rheumatoid arthritis, melatonin is not recommended.

Omegas

Omegas are fatty acids. Fatty acids are known as "essential" fats because the body needs them to build healthy cells and keep the brain and nervous system functioning properly. Omegas come in three types: omega-3, omega-6, and omega-9. In this section, you'll discover how taking omega supplements may help reduce symptoms of executive dysfunction. Omega supplements have been found to be somewhat effective in treating ADHD, may tend to cause fewer side effects than stimulant medication, and may even help reduce side effects from stimulant medication (Barragán, Breuer, and Döpfner, 2014; Bader and Adesman, 2012).

Omega-3

Omega-3 is known as a highly unsaturated fatty acid (HUFA). HUFAs are healthy kinds of fat. Omega-3 has been found to lower blood fat, help with arthritis, improve heart health, decrease depression, aid in fetal development, decrease asthma symptoms, improve ADHD symptoms, and improve dementia (Hunt and McManus, 2014; Peter, Chopra, and Jacob, 2013). Omega-3 fatty acids come in three different types: eicosapentaenoic acid (EPA), docosahexaenoic acid (DHA), and alpha-linolenic acid (ALA). EPA and DHA are usually found in fish, while ALA is found in nuts and seeds. EPA, DHA, and ALA are not manufactured naturally in the body, so they are obtained through food or supplements. Foods that are rich in omegas include nuts, vegetables, and fish.

When individuals have low omega-3 levels in their blood, they can exhibit similar symptoms to those found in ADHD, such as inattention, lack of focus, mood swings, and working memory problems (Montgomery, Burton, Sewell, Spreckelsen, and Richardson, 2013). Indeed, some studies have found that individuals with ADHD exhibit significantly lower levels of omega-3 fatty acids in their blood than those without ADHD (Hawkey and Nigg, 2014; Schuchardt et al., 2010; Antalis et al., 2006). Omega-3, omega-6, and omega-9 have been found to boost this low level of omegas in the blood and improve ADHD symptoms (Hawkey and Nigg, 2014; Nguyen et al., 2014; Huss, Volp, and Stauss-Grabo, 2009; Sinn, Bryan, and Wilson, 2008; Sinn and Bryan, 2007; Joshi et al., 2006; Young et al., 2005).

One study found that omega-3 significantly increased EF performance in older adults compared to those taking a placebo (Witte et al., 2013). Omega-3 was also found to be helpful in improving processing speed and attention among individuals with age-related cognitive decline, although this same effect was not observed among those with Alzheimer's Disease (Mazereeuw, Lanctôt, Chau, Swardfager, and Herrmann, 2012). Omega-3 may help neurons communicate more effectively, as seen on brain scans (Bauer et al., 2014; Gow and Hibbeln, 2014). In some cases, this effect on neural efficiency can be seen after four weeks of taking omega-3 supplements (Bauer et al., 2014).

Omega-6 and omega-9 is also found in poultry and whole-grain bread. Some studies find that omega-6 helps improve EFs such as emotion regulation, inhibition, and self-regulation (Hawkey and Nigg, 2014; Nguyen et al., 2014; Huss, Volp, and Stauss-Grabo, 2009; Sinn, Bryan, and Wilson, 2008; Sinn and Bryan, 2007; Joshi et al., 2006; Young et al., 2005)

Omega-9

Omega-9 can be found in animal fat and vegetable oil. It can also be found in olive oil, macadamia oil, and mustard seed. While you don't see omega-9 as much in ADHD omega studies as omega-3 and omega-6, it has been found to help improve EFs such as emotion regulation, inhibition, and self-regulation (Hawkey and Nigg, 2014; Nguyen et al., 2014; Huss, Volp, and Stauss-Grabo, 2009; Sinn, Bryan, and Wilson, 2008; Sinn and Bryan, 2007; Joshi et al., 2006; Young et al., 2005).

Side Effects of Omegas

Omegas can act as blood thinners (anticoagulants). Just like with any supplement, it is very important that you and your client have open communication with his prescriber before taking omegas. This is especially true if your client is taking blood-thinning medications like Coumadin (warfarin). Omegas can also cause stomach upset.

One of the other side effects of taking omegas is a "fish burp" after taking fish oil omegas. This is exactly what it sounds like – a burp that tastes like fish. Options to avoid fish burp include buying enteric-coated omegas, as enteric-coated omegas have a thicker covering to the omega capsule. However, because of this thicker covering, enteric-coated omegas are more expensive than their non-coated counterparts. Liquid versions of fish oil may also help reduce fish burp. There are also non-fish oil options for omega supplements such as flax seed oil and chia. For more information on omegas, see the Resources section at the end of this workbook.

TIPS

The Placebo Effect

It would be remiss to speak about medications and supplements without bringing up the very powerful nature of the placebo effect. When you review medication and supplement studies, note how much of an effect is due to the medication or supplement, and how much is a result of the placebo effect. Just the fact that a person is talking with a clinician about his issue has a curative effect. A recent study found that even if you tell a person that they are getting a placebo pill they will get better (Caravalho, Caetano, Cunha, Rebouta, Kaptchuk, and Kirsch, 2016).

In addition, the placebo effect is so powerful that the FDA requires a *placebo-controlled double-blind study* in order for a medication to qualify for approval. This means that the study subject taking the drug doesn't know if it's active or placebo, the study physician prescribing the drug doesn't know if it's active or placebo, and the clinician rating the study subject's behavior from visit to visit doesn't know if the drug is active or placebo. The fact that no one knows what each study subject is taking significantly helps reduce study bias.

So keep in mind when working with clients that medication and supplements may seem like they're working, but the results could be, at least in part, due to the placebo effect. An example of the placebo effect would be having a headache and within five minutes of taking ibuprofen your headache goes away. You've experienced the placebo effect, as ibuprofen does not work that rapidly.

CHAPTER 4 Therapy Techniques

In this chapter you will read about one of the most effective psychotherapies for executive dysfunction – cognitive-behavioral therapy (CBT). You will discover CBT concepts such as "cognitive distortions" and "negative cognitions," as well as CBT techniques such as thought stopping and reframing. You will discover about the benefits of CBT in individual, group, couples, and family counseling. You will learn issues specific to couples where one or both of the partners has executive dysfunction EF issues. You will learn about social skills issues and how prevalent they are for your clients with EF issues. You will learn techniques for helping your client improve social interactions with others and decreasing social anxiety. From reading this chapter you will also discover how to teach your client with executive dysfunction how to judge a healthy relationship from an unhealthy one, and how to practice good social reciprocity. You will also learn about an intervention referred to as "coaching." It's not therapy, but it may help your client improve his goal-setting, prioritizing, and organizing. Since coaching is not licensed or certified in any state, you will find questions your client should ask a coach before hiring one.

COGNITIVE-BEHAVIORAL THERAPY

Cognitive-behavioral therapy (CBT) is a therapeutic treatment that focuses on helping identify faulty cognitions and cognitive distortions. It is one of the therapies you will see most often in research. CBT is applicable in individual, group, couples, and family therapy. It has the most evidence of any therapeutic technique in successfully improving executive function impairment. For individuals with ADHD in particular, studies have found that CBT is effective in treating symptoms both in the short-term and long-term.

TENETS OF CBT

A Greek philosopher named Epictetus once wrote, "People are not disturbed by things, but by the views they take of them." This is an excellent illustration of three principles behind CBT:

- The way a person thinks about something can change outcomes.
- People can become aware of and change the way they think.
- Changing one's thinking can change one's behavior.

(Beck, 2011; Blagys and Hilsenroth, 2002)

In CBT, it is believed that a person's dysfunctional thinking about an event and consequent behavior in response to that thinking has more of an impact on his wellbeing than the event itself (Beck, 2011). CBT focuses on changing these negative thoughts or attitudes to more positive, healthy ones (Scott and Freeman, 2010).

COGNITIVE-BEHAVIOR THERAPY CONCEPTS

CBT concepts include thought-stopping and cognitive distortions. Cognitive distortions include catastrophizing, minimizing, overgeneralizing, and personalizing.

The following handouts will help teach your clients how CBT works:

- How Cognitive-Behavioral Therapy Works
- Learning Thought-Stopping
- Cognitive Distortions
- Identifying Cognitive Distortions

How Cognitive-Behavioral Therapy Works

A view of one of the tenets of CBT would look something like this:

ACTION → BELIEF → CONSEQUENCE

You experience an event, then you have a thought or belief about that event. This leads to a consequence, or result. In CBT, you focus on changing the faulty "belief" part of this process. For example, one day on the way to work you step in a mud puddle. You say to yourself, "I can't believe I was so stupid. Everyone is going to laugh at me at the office." You end up having a bad day.

Let's improve that belief process. You step in a mud puddle on your way to work. You say to yourself, "Geez, I guess this just happens sometimes. I'll have a good story for my coworkers." You end up laughing about the puddle, and you have a pretty good day. CBT helps change the unhelpful (and even detrimental) beliefs into ones which result in happier and healthier choices.

77

Learning Thought-Stopping

Sometimes when you are presented with a new project at work, you may have thoughts of "I can't do this," "I'm stupid," or "I never get projects done." When you have a negative thought, visualize a stop sign popping up. Now replace that thought with a positive one. Replace "I can't do this" with "I am smart and capable." Here is the process of "thought-stopping" broken into steps:

1. Recognize the negative thought. Become aware that you are being tough on yourself and that it is not helpful or healthy.

2. Visualize a red stop sign popping up and blocking that negative thought. You can also say to yourself, "Stop," "That's negative, change that," "That is not healthy or helpful," or any other phrase that acknowledges the negative thought and reminds you to stay positive and in the present.

3. Create a positive phrase to replace the negative one. For example, if you are meeting a new group of people, turn the negative thought of "They're going to think I'm weird" into the positive thought of "I'm confident, have good social skills, and I'll enjoy meeting these new people." Keep in mind that you want to avoid using "not" in the positive phrase. Turn it around into something more positive. For example, "I'm not going to screw this up" can be rephrased into "I'm going to do just fine."

The more you practice replacing your negative thoughts with positive ones, the more likely your mind will automatically go to a positive thought.

Identifying Negative Thoughts

If you're not sure if your self-talk is negative, ask yourself the following questions about your thoughts, using the acronym **THINK**:

1. It is **T**houghtful?
2. Is it **H**elpful?
3. Is it **I**nspiring?
4. Is it **N**eeded?
5. Is it **K**ind?

If you can't answer "yes" to one or more of these questions, you may have a negative thought on your hands. Time to practice some positive thought replacement and reframing. The THINK questions are also helpful to run through when you are communicating in a relationship and want to watch what you say.

Cognitive Distortions

Sometimes a person has "cognitive distortions" – ways of thinking that just aren't logical or helpful. Cognitive distortions include catastrophizing, minimizing, overgeneralization, and personalization.

CATASTROPHIZING

When you catastrophize, you are "making a mountain out of a molehill." This means that you are making something into a much bigger deal than it actually is. An example of catastrophizing is being given a new assignment at work, and all of the sudden you are convinced that you will fail at the assignment, lose your job, and be living on the street. In reality, you were just handed the assignment five minutes ago.

MINIMIZING

Minimizing is the opposite of catastrophizing, but it is just as much of a distortion of thinking. Instead of making a mountain out of a molehill, you are making a molehill out of a mountain. It is interpreting important things as not being a big deal. For example, your friends and family tell you that they think you are drinking too much. You respond that it's just a few beers after work, and you are just fine.

OVERGENERALIZING

Overgeneralizing happens when you come up with a conclusion based on very little information. Usually people tend to overgeneralize in response to a situation that is not in their favor. (Funny how that works, isn't it?) An example of overgeneralization would be if your friend calls the day she was supposed to go shopping with you and tells you she can't make it. In response, you automatically think you have no friends.

PERSONALIZING

In life, very rarely are events personal. This means that the things that happen to you in life are usually not a personal attack on you or what you perceive to be "bad luck." In reality, things sometimes just happen. Similar to overgeneralizing, when you personalize, the conclusion you formulate in your head tends not to work in your favor. An example of personalization would be when you call a friend, and they sound distant. You think, "I must have done something wrong to upset him. He's saying he's fine, but I'm sure he's mad at me." In reality, you don't know why he sounds distant. It could be for a variety of reasons, and chances are those reasons have nothing to do with you.

Identifying Cognitive Distortions

For the following statements, identify whether it is an example of catastrophizing, minimizing, overgeneralizing, or personalizing.

1. The cashier didn't say hello. She must think I'm not worthy of her attention.

_____

_____

_____

2. I caught my son smoking marijuana again. I guess this is just something teenagers do.

_____

_____

_____

3. I got a poor performance review. I'm just going to get poor performance reviews from here on out.

_____

_____

_____

4. I got a B on this report. I'm going to fail out of graduate school for sure.

_____

_____

_____

5. I just tripped in front of people. Nothing goes well in my life.

_____

_____

_____

REFRAMING

In CBT, reframing involves taking a cognitive distortion and turning it into a positive thought. If you don't know the reason for something, why not create a reason that is in your favor instead of having it work against you?

Staying Away from Absolutes

In general, it helps to stay away from using words such as "always" and "never" in self-talk or when talking to others. Usually a discussion with a partner where "always" and "never" are involved doesn't end well. For example, "You always interrupt me," or "You never take the trash out." Very rarely in life are things absolute, all or nothing – they are shades of gray. Cutting out all-or-nothing words (along with all-or-nothing thinking) can help your client feel more at ease with themselves and with others.

Working on Reframing

For each of the following statements, come up with a positive reframe.

1. I'm never going to get this work done.

_____

2. Bad things always happen to me.

_____

3. My partner and I always fight.

_____

4. If I eat this cookie, my entire diet is blown.

_____

5. My day is already ruined.

_____

6. I'm a bad driver.

_____

7. I don't even want to try to do this project.

_____

8. My life is so boring and uneventful.

_____

9. I'd start a new hobby, but it's so expensive.

_____

10. My worrying will never stop.

_____

Reframing Negative Cognitions

Practice replacing your negative cognitions with positive ones. If you don't know the outcome of something, why not tell yourself things that work in your favor.

1. Your thought: _____I'M NEVER GOING TO GET THIS DONE_____
    Turn it into a positive: ___I AM SMART, CAPABLE, AND CAN GET THIS DONE ON TIME_____

2. Your thought: _____
    Turn it into a positive: _____

3. Your thought: _____
    Turn it into a positive: _____

4. Your thought: _____
    Turn it into a positive: _____

5. Your thought: _____
    Turn it into a positive: _____

6. Your thought: _____
    Turn it into a positive: _____

7. Your thought: _____
    Turn it into a positive: _____

8. Your thought: _____
    Turn it into a positive: _____

9. Your thought: _____
    Turn it into a positive: _____

10. Your thought: _____
    Turn it into a positive: _____

Anxiety Hierarchy

In an anxiety hierarchy activity, you work with your client in identifying the most anxiety-provoking events and labeling them with a number from 100 (most anxiety-provoking) to 0 (not anxiety-provoking). You start by listing the most anxiety-provoking event first.

The purpose of the hierarchy is to help your client distinguish the severity of anxiety connected to each anxiety-provoking event. When clients encounter anxiety, it can feel like a big wall, with each event as provoking as the next. If you are trained in exposure therapy, an anxiety hierarchy can give you a good framework for treatment.

Rating	Fear/Anxiety
100	Speaking in front of a group of strangers
95	Being asked a question during a staff meeting

TYPES OF COGNITIVE-BEHAVIORAL THERAPY

CBT is used in the following formats: individual therapy, group therapy, and couples therapy. While individual therapy can be helpful, there may be some advantages to CBT in a group setting. When a person is in group therapy, he experiences the concept of *universality*. This is a very powerful motivator and factor in healing. This is the realization that you are not the only one with a particular issue (Beiling, McCabe, and Antony, 2013). In addition, in group therapy, clients get encouragement from the members of the group. One of the biggest things a group can give a client is hope and confidence, as well as encouragement in achieving goals (Solanto, 2012). Members of the group also hold each other accountable for completing CBT homework and group attendance – and being held accountable is a powerful motivator. It has been found that the greater the number of weekly home exercises completed by a CBT group participant, the greater the overall benefit he gets from the group (Solanto, 2012).

Benefits of CBT Group Therapy Over Other Therapies

People with executive dysfunction may be more likely to attend CBT group therapy on a more regular basis than regular therapy or a support group. For example, in one study, 28% of those attending an ADHD support group missed three or more sessions, compared to only 13% of those enrolled a CBT group. Moreover, individuals in the support group did not see the same amount of positive change that they did in the cognitive-behavior group (Solanto, 2012). In a study by Safren et al. (2010), 53% of adults with ADHD who received 12 sessions of individual CBT had significant improvements in their symptoms compared to 23% who only received relaxation training and educational support. The CBT group continued to show improvement six months and 12 months after treatment.

CBT COUPLES THERAPY

Couples where one or both partners have executive dysfunction have unique issues that other couples don't face. They have much more stress and exhibit different ways of dealing with stress than other couples (Overby, Snell, and Callis, 2011). Among individuals with ADHD in particular, there is a higher rate of divorce and remarriage compared to the general population (Klein et al., 2012; Barkley, Murphy, and Fischer, 2008). In addition, individuals with executive dysfunction, particularly ADHD, and their partners report more martial dissatisfaction and problems in their marriage than those without ADHD (Eakin et al., 2004; Minde et al., 2003).

The two biggest causes of arguments amongst couples are sex and money. These issues are amplified when one or both partners have EF issues. The impulsive nature of executive dysfunction makes a person more likely to be irresponsible with money or exhibit risky sexual behavior (Garcia, MacKillop, Aller, Merriwether, Wilson, and Lum, 2010; Sarkis and Klein, 2009; Barkley et al., 2008). You will learn more about financial issues and executive dysfunction in Chapter 9. If one member of a couple will not attend therapy, it is recommended that the other partner attends on their own.

Issues of Couples with Executive Dysfunction

Issues that couples with executive dysfunction face more than other couples include:

- Lack of sex drive or excessive sex drive.
- Infidelity.
- Not keeping track of purchases.
- Disagreements on setting limits their children.
- Hiding purchases from partner/spouse.
- Impulsive spending.
- Difficulty focusing during sex.
- Disliking repetitive touch.
- "Flying off the handle" and having a "short fuse."
- Disorganized in the home and creating clutter.
- Not having an emergency fund.
- Addiction to pornography.
- Not picking up their children on time from school or after-school activities.
- Not following through on household chores.
- Not appearing to listen when spoken to.
- Disorganization of financial papers.
- Addiction to gambling.
- Waiting until the last minute to make reservations for a family vacation (Garcia et al., 2010; Barkley et al., 2008).

SOCIAL SKILLS

Many people with EF difficulties have issues with social skills – difficulty reading nonverbal cues, difficulty interrupting, or even standing too close to their conversation partner. CBT has shown effectiveness in helping people with executive dysfunction grow and practice their social skills (Emilsson et al., 2011). Social skills training can be provided in individual or group counseling. In this section, you will learn techniques to help your clients improve their social skills. For more information on social skills issues, see the Resources section at the end of this workbook.

Social Anxiety

When a person is prone to interrupting or talking excessively during social interactions, there is a tendency to start self-monitoring so as to not make social errors. However, this self-monitoring can turn into social anxiety. A person becomes so aware of their tendency for making social errors that they limit their social contact and monitor themselves into silence. Role-plays and CBT have been found to be quite effective for treating social anxiety, along with the use of anxiolytic and antidepressant medication.

EXERCISE

Social Role-Plays

Role-plays are a great way to practice social skills in the comfort of the therapist's office. When clients act out a social situation, particularly a social situation that has previously caused anxiety or stress, it bolsters confidence. Consider doing role-plays such as:

- Talking with a supervisor about a promotion or raise.
- Introducing himself/herself to a new person.
- Talking with a coworker about concerns regarding a project.
- Inviting a friend to an event.

During role-plays, you act as the authority, and the client plays himself or herself. One of the "rules" of role-plays is that you have to act "as if" you are that person. Acting "as if" lets a client's defenses come down more easily. For example, instead of saying, "The boss would say this," you speak as if you are actually the boss. Switch roles and practice the role-play again. When the client acts as the authority figure, you can see more of what the client is afraid might happen in that social situation. When you have explored a variety of outcomes in a social situation, it greatly reduces your client's anxiety.

EXERCISE

The Hula-Hoop Technique

When people have EF difficulties, sometimes they stand too close or too far away when they are engaged in conversation. One way to practice appropriate conversational distance is by holding a hula-hoop between you and your client when you are engaging in role-plays. The width of a hula-hoop equates to standard conversational distance in the U.S. A visible, tangible way to remember skills, such as a hula-hoop, helps your client remember those skills and apply them for later use. As a bonus, hula-hoops are inexpensive and easily available, so this is a great technique for your client to practice with trusted friends and family outside of sessions.

EXERCISE # Teaching Nonverbal Signals

As you read earlier, people with EF difficulties have issues monitoring their social behavior. It makes them tired and socially anxious to constantly monitor if they are doing the "right" social behaviors. To help your client relax and enjoy a group social situation, a nonverbal "signal" can be worked out between your client and a trusted friend or family member.

In group social situations, nonverbal signals can let your client know when they are interrupting or rambling on – without making it obvious to the other people in the social setting. As you read earlier in the workbook, people with executive dysfunction may have anxiety – and in particular social anxiety. By worrying about how they are perceived socially, people with social anxiety actually make more social mistakes. As the saying goes, what you focus on grows. A way to help take the pressure off a person with executive dysfunction is to work out a nonverbal cue system at social events.

Have your client and a friend or family member create a nonverbal signal for each social situation, like a tug on the ear if your client interrupts or a scratch on the head if your client rambles on.

Practice these signals with your client and their trusted friend or family member in your office, to make sure everyone is in agreement on the signals. This is a good way for the person with EF difficulties to not have to monitor their behavior so much – now someone else is helping them.

Many people with EF difficulties have noticed that when they have someone with them cuing them, they make fewer social errors because they are more relaxed.

Social skills issues where a nonverbal signal can be useful:

- Interrupting
- Rambling
- Standing too close
- Needing to take a break
- Standing too far away
- Asking inappropriate (too personal) questions

Nonverbal signals include:

- Tugging the ear
- Scratching the head
- Coughing
- Making a subtle "wrap it up" signal with the hand
- Touching hand to the chin
- Breaking off and going to the side of the room (this gives your client an "easy out" from a conversation)

Apologizing Properly

When you have executive function (EF) difficulties, you may be finding yourself upsetting people because you don't have as much of a "filter" when you talk to others. You may also tend to show up late for significant events. Some people may be very open about telling you that you have upset them.

Keep in mind that having EF difficulties does not give you a "free pass" – you still need to own the behavior and apologize if you've hurt someone. There are different types of apologies. For example:

"I'm sorry you got upset when I forgot to take the trash out."

This type of apology blames the other person, instead of you taking responsibility for your behavior. Instead, a proper apology is the following:

"I'm sorry I forgot to take the trash out. I'm putting a timer on my phone for next week when I should put the cans at the curb."

You are acknowledging the behavior, telling the person that you are sorry that you upset them, and then adding how you're working on improving the behavior in the future.

Practice writing an apology for a recent event where you hurt someone's feelings.

_____

_____

_____

_____

_____

_____

_____

_____

_____

_____

Using "I Feel" Statements

Let's say a friend or family member has done something that upsets you. There is a way to address your concern in a respectful and assertive way. This is accomplished using "I feel" statements. In "I feel" statements, you are stating the behavior that bothered you, how it made you feel, and why.

Note that you didn't use the word "you" in that sentence. When you say, "When you didn't put the trash can at the curb…" the other person tends to get defensive. For an added bonus, you can add, "How can we work together to make this better?" at the end of your "I feel" statement. This helps the person see that you are willing to work together as a team.

Now try creating your own "I feel" statements:

Example:

1. When ___THE TRASH CAN ISN'T AT THE CURB ON WEDNESDAYS_____

   happens I feel ___FRUSTRATED___ because ___THE TRASH CAN IS ALREADY FULL FOR THE NEXT WEEK___.

2. When _____ happens I feel

   _____ because _____.

3. When _____ happens I feel

   _____ because _____.

4. When _____ happens I feel

   _____ because _____.

Do You Have a Healthy Relationship/Friendship?

Answer the following questions to determine if a relationship or friendship is good for you:

- Can you count on this person in emergencies?

  _____

  _____

- Do you feel like this person really listens to you?

  _____

  _____

- Does this person speak respectfully to you?

  _____

  _____

- Do you feel that you both have equal power or "say" in the relationship?

  _____

  _____

- Are you getting your needs (respect, comfort, understanding) met in the relationship?

  _____

  _____

- Does this person keep your private information to himself or herself?

  _____

  _____

- Does this person respect your boundaries (what you are okay and not okay with)?

  _____

  _____

If you answered "no" to any of these questions, consider whether the relationship is a healthy one. Consider talking it over with your counselor or a trusted friend or family member.

How to "Rebalance" a Relationship

If you find that you've been doing a lot of "taking" in a relationship and not much giving, here are some ways to rebalance your relationship:

• Tell the person face-to-face how much you appreciate what he has done for you.

• Send a card to the person.

• Take the person out to lunch or dinner.

• Offer to run an errand for him or her.

• Offer to watch the kids so your partner can take a break.

• The next time you go to the movies, buy the person's ticket.

• Ask the person if there is anything you can do for them.

• If you see something at the store that you think they might like, buy it for them.

Know Your Rights

Sometimes when life has been rough, it can be easy to forget what your rights are as a person. It helps to know these rights so you can practice speaking up for yourself. As a person, you have a right to:

- Say "no" at any time

- Say "no" without an explanation

- Change your mind at any time

- Feel safe, physically and emotionally

- Express your feelings

- Walk away from a situation

Keep these rights in mind when you start feeling anxious about a situation or are talking to someone about your needs. Listen to your intuition or instincts. That feeling in your gut will tell you if you are in a safe situation or not.

What are some situations where you could change your situation by relying on these rights?

_____

_____

_____

_____

_____

_____

_____

The "Sunk Cost Fallacy"

As humans, when we've invested our time and energy in something, we are much more likely to put in more time and energy than "cut our losses" and walk away. This is true of investing, of jobs, and of relationships. This is called the "sunk cost fallacy," originally used in behavioral economics (formerly known as consumer psychology). People may hang on to relationships because they feel that ending the relationship would mean they "wasted time" with their partner. If a person has EF difficulties, they may feel even more so that they "need" their partner in their life, as that person may provide stability, organization, or even financial support to them.

Reframe the ending of a relationship as a time of growth. Yes, there is loss, but also discuss what your client learned and how they grew from this relationship. Explain the concept of the "sunk cost fallacy" and how it is a natural part of being human. When it is presented as a normal feeling people go through, it may give your client the push they need to either break free from the relationship or take time to reassess. (That's another issue when clients have executive dysfunction – they tend to start and end relationships quickly, due to the excitement and flood of feel-good brain chemicals.)

What are some areas in which your clients may experience "sunk costs"?

1. _____

_____

2. _____

_____

3. _____

_____

4. _____

_____

5. _____

_____

6. _____

_____

Ending an Unhealthy Relationship

You may have discovered that the relationship you're in is no longer healthy for you or you have "outgrown" the relationship. Sometimes when you start getting help for your issues, the *dynamic* in your relationship, or how your relationships work, changes. This can sometimes lead to realizing that your needs aren't being met in a relationship. When this happens, sometimes breakups are inevitable. Keep in mind during a breakup that your feelings of loss are temporary. There is a Buddhist saying that "pain is inevitable, but suffering is optional." A book that is recommended if you are going through a breakup is *Surviving the Loss of a Love* by Peter McWilliams. Remember that you have grown and learned from this relationship.

If you've decided that you need to end your relationship, be kind but direct. If you do not make it clear that you are ending the relationship, your partner may get the message that you have not truly decided on the fate of the relationship and may mistakenly believe that there is a chance you can work things out. Here are some general guidelines when ending a relationship:

- Meet in a neutral public location, like a coffee shop or a park.
- Meet somewhere that does not have any emotional meaning to you, such as a place where you met, or a place you drive by or walk by frequently.
- Take your own car.
- State that things are not working out anymore in the relationship, and you've grown apart.
- Avoid making comments of "maybe someday it will work", or "I need a break" just to soothe hurt feelings.
- If your former partner asks repeatedly why you are ending the relationship, repeat that the two of you have just grown apart, and it is no one's fault.
- Keep the meeting short, and excuse yourself if your voices start rising in volume or if you feel you may have an anger outburst.
- Expect your former partner to be upset. However, any reaction of physical abuse, threats to harm you or your family, or threats to harm himself should be reported to 911 and legal authorities immediately.

If you are ending a friendship, you can follow a similar pattern, although sometimes just having less contact is a way of ending your friendship. Limited contact may be the best option if you are decreasing your involvement with a family member or coworker – someone you may still see often.

In addition, before you decide to end a relationship, realize that you may be prone to making impulsive decisions. You also may become bored easily in relationships once the initial sparks wear off (this "romantic phase" of a relationship lasts six months to a year). Think about whether the reason you want to end the relationship is fixable. Are you happier with the person or without them? In some cases, counseling can help a couple heal their relationship, and it can also help them have a healthy breakup.

COACHING

While coaching is not a type of therapy, it does involve helping clients with executive dysfunction.

Coaches can help with:

- Organization skills
- Setting up a structured schedule
- Establishing priorities for tasks
- Creating goals for work and home life
- Formulating realistic steps or objectives for goals
- Accountability for completing projects or assignments

With accountability, clients will check in with a coach when a work assignment is completed. A client may even "turn in" their work to a coach to show proof of completion. Having an accountability partner is very important for people with executive dysfunction. As humans, we like being *socially consistent* - doing what we say we're going to do. This means that if your client's coach knows they have an assignment due that week, your client is much more likely to complete that assignment. To do otherwise would risk being seen as socially inconsistent.

Questions to Ask a Prospective Coach

If you are considering hiring a coach, you should ask him the following questions:

- What is his educational background?

- What licenses and/or certifications does he hold?

- What experience does he have with ADHD and other executive function-related disorders?

- How long has he been in business?

- What are some strategies he uses?

- What does he believe about a person's ability to change?

- What does he charge?

- Is he available in person, over the phone, via text, or via video conferencing?

- How often are coaching appointments? (It's usually once a week.)

- Does he charge for questions you may have between appointments?

- Does he let clients text and email him between sessions at no charge for accountability in turning in assignments?

- How long does he expect coaching to last? (Coaching is supposed to be a brief intervention – the coach teaches you skills, checks to see if you have mastered those skills, and is available for periodic check-ins as needed after that.)

Make sure the coach's views line up with yours, and pay attention to your intuition. If something doesn't feel right, it probably isn't. A coach is not supposed to talk about any psychological issues or about your family – especially if they are not licensed or certified. If they do so and they are not a licensed clinician, they are breaking the law.

CHAPTER 5 Mindfulness Meditation

In this chapter, you will read about the difference between meditation and mindfulness meditation. You will discover how studies have shown that mindfulness meditation has helped people with executive dysfunction have happier and less stressful lives. You will also learn mindfulness practices you can teach your clients. Mindfulness meditation is one of the ideal treatments addressed in this workbook, since there is data supporting its efficacy, a person doesn't need training to do it, they don't need any extra equipment, it doesn't cost anything, and it can be done anywhere.

Individuals who practice mind-body interventions on a regular basis, like "standard" meditation and mindfulness meditation, have a significantly lower level of cortisol in their system than people who do not practice them (Iglesias, Azzara, Granchetti, Lagomarsino, and Vigo, 2014). You learned about cortisol in Chapter 2 when you read about oppositional defiant disorder (ODD). Cortisol is a hormone that the sympathetic (fight, flight or freeze) part of your autonomic nervous system releases when you are under stress. Chronic release of cortisol can increase your chances of developing heart disease and other illnesses. Meditation and mindfulness meditation are relatively simple practices that lead to big health benefits, such as reducing depression and anxiety (Parswani, Sharma, and Iyengar, 2013).

Meditation is directly correlated with reductions in executive function (EF) impairment. In Chapter 1, you learned about the prefrontal cortex "housing" the executive functions. It should come as no surprise that individuals who meditate regularly have more developed regions of the brain involved in processes such as attention, self-monitoring, and emotional processing compared to those who do not meditate (Lazar, Kerr, Wasserman, Gray, Greve, and Treadway, et al., 2005).

MEDITATION

In essence, meditation involves focusing on your breathing. You either sit or lie down during meditation. Two types of meditation include "focused attention" and "open monitoring" (Travis and Shear, 2010). Each of these types of meditation can impact how the brain functions. In focused attention meditation, you focus on an image, object, or sound while you are meditating. For example, you can repeat a phrase to yourself or look at a relaxing picture while you meditate. You will learn about a form of open monitoring meditation called mindfulness meditation in the next section.

In some forms of meditation, you sit in a chair with your eyes closed. The goal is to achieve a state of "restful alertness." This means you are in deep rest but are also alert. One study found a significant improvement in ADHD symptoms and executive functioning, as well as a decrease in levels of stress and anxiety, after meditation was practiced twice a day (Grosswald, Stixrud, Travis, and Bateh, 2008).

Are You Trying to Empty Your Mind?

The goal of meditation is to stay in the "here and now," or present. The goal is not to totally empty your mind. Even individuals who have been practicing meditation for several years find it difficult to totally empty their minds. If you have a thought float into your mind, you acknowledge that thought, and let it float on out.

Having thoughts float in and out during meditation is referred to as "monkey brain." It is called monkey brain because as you meditate you can have thoughts swing in and out of your mind just like a monkey jumps from branch to branch (Mikulas, 2014). You can especially have monkey brain if you have executive dysfunction. For this reason, standard meditation can be challenging for people with EF difficulties, and they may be able to meditate for only brief periods of time. Mindfulness meditation is a more user-friendly way of meditating for individuals with EF difficulties.

MINDFULNESS MEDITATION

In mindfulness meditation, distractions are actually welcomed. This can bring a sigh of relief from people with executive dysfunction, since standard meditation can be frustrating for them. People with EF difficulties tend to be unnecessarily hard on themselves when they don't get a practice "right" the first few times, so mindfulness meditation can be a welcome change and a successful way to meditate. While mindfulness is a form of meditation, not all meditation is mindfulness (Zylowska, 2012). Mindfulness meditation is a form of "open monitoring" meditation in that you are aware of your thoughts, as opposed to standard meditation where you block out distractions (Chiesa and Malinowski, 2011).

When you practice mindfulness, you are fully focused on your activity in the moment. Mindfulness is defined as paying attention to present experience (Smalley, Loo, Hale, Shrestha, McGough, Flook, and Reise, 2009). You are staying in the "here and now." Staying in the here and now can help improve executive dysfunction, particularly with regard to issues such as impulsivity and self-regulation. As you learned in Chapter 1, self-regulation is the brain's ability to realize it is off-task and bring itself back – without a person even being aware of this phenomenon taking place. Mindfulness can also help with self-awareness and managing executive dysfunction symptoms, such as difficulties with attention and emotion regulation. Mindfulness can also help people become more accepting and positive with themselves and others (Zylowska, 2012).

Mindfulness has also been found to improve attention, regulate emotions, and improve social relationships (Zylowska, Ackerman, Yang, Futrell, Horton, Hale, Pataki, and Smalley, 2008). It also can significantly reduce anxiety and depression symptoms, perceived stress, blood pressure, and even decrease weight in people who have heart disease (Parswani, Sharma, and Iyengar, 2013).

When individuals with executive dysfunction experience challenges practicing mindfulness, it is usually due to deficits in self-regulation coupled with increased novelty-seeking (Smalley et al., 2009). As you learned earlier in the workbook, novelty-seeking leads to people with executive dysfunction being distracted by new things and seeking new stimulation.

Mindfulness in a Group Setting

Mindfulness group training includes relaxation techniques, focusing on breathing, using mental imagery, and becoming aware of the body and mind (Chiesa and Malinowski, 2011). Typically, group mindfulness training lasts 8 to 10 weeks. For people with executive function issues, 8 to 10 weeks is enough time to learn the necessary skills without becoming overwhelmed or burned out.

One study found that after an eight-week mindfulness training group, adults with ADHD exhibited a significant improvement in both self- and clinician-rated ADHD symptoms and EF performance, including emotion regulation (Mitchell, McIntyre, English, Dennis, Beckham, and Kollins, 2013). Similarly, another study found that teenagers and adults who participated in an eight-week mindfulness group showed significant improvements in self-ratings of ADHD, depression, anxiety, and stress, as well as improved performance on tests of attention and inhibition. These improvements continued even three months after the training group (Zylowska et al., 2008).

Changes in the gray matter (i.e., cerebral cortex) of the brain have also been observed following mindfulness training, with evidence for changes in regions of the brain involved in learning, memory, processing emotions, thinking about the self, and ability to take different perspectives (Zylowska, 2012; Hölzel, Carmody, Vangel, Congleton, Yerramsetti, Gard, and Lazar, 2010). It is important to continue practicing mindfulness in order to maintain its benefits, as another study found that the effects of a mindfulness training program decreased eight weeks after the training ended (Weijer-Bergsma, Formsma, Bruin, and Bögels, 2012).

Mindfulness may also help with parenting skills. One study looked at the effects of a mindful parent training group for parents of children with ADHD and found evidence that parents who participated in the group reported a significant reduction in their own ADHD symptoms, as well as a significant reduction in parenting stress and overreacting to their child's behavior (van der Oord, Bogels, and Peijnenburg, 2012).

Mindfulness and Distraction

Lidia Zylowska, MD (2012), a psychiatrist and researcher in mindfulness meditation, says that you don't have to empty your mind to practice mindfulness. Mindfulness is more about observing your mind. The more mindfulness practice you do, the more your mind may quiet down. However, even if you have difficulty quieting your mind you can still have a positive mindfulness experience. In fact, in mindfulness meditation, distractions are actually *welcomed*. One of the ideas behind mindfulness is that you practice it where you're going to use it. This is called *context-dependent learning*. So being distracted and active is actually a bonus when you are practicing mindfulness! Move around all you want. Dr. Zylowska says you do need to practice mindfulness at least three times a week to receive benefits. This isn't that much, considering you can do a simple mindfulness task in a few minutes.

The following handouts provide simple mindfulness practices that your clients can use.

Use STOP to Practice Mindfulness

STOP is an acronym that can help you practice mindfulness during your day (Zylowska, 2012).

S = Stop (or pause) for a moment

T = Take a deep breath

O = Observe mindfully in the moment (notice your body sensations or what you are doing)

P = Proceed with relaxation and awareness

On the "Proceed" step, this is your chance to change your actions if you find yourself being distracted or avoiding a task. It can be difficult to make those choices, but the more you practice and use mindfulness with other treatments, the easier it becomes (Zylowska, 2012).

Walking Mindfulness Practice

A great way to practice mindfulness meditation is by taking a walk. You don't need any extra equipment or training – all you need is a pair of comfortable shoes. You can go for a walk in any environment and practice mindfulness meditation. Mindful walking has been found to significantly reduce psychological stress and improve quality of life (Teut, Roesner, Ortiz, Reese, Binting, and Roll, et al., 2013). The mindfulness practice you'll learn about in this exercise can be found in Buddhist monk Thich Nhat Hanh's work *Peace is Every Step: The Path of Mindfulness in Every Day Life* (1991).

- Walk outside at a slower pace than usual

- Focus on how your body feels as you walk

  - Focus on the sensation of your feet on the ground

  - Focus on the feeling of the breeze on your face

  - Focus on the temperature of the air

  - Focus on your breathing

    – Take three steps with each inhale and three steps with each exhale

    – Say "in" to yourself when inhaling and "out" as you exhale, to help keep track of your breathing

- If you see something beautiful, like a tree, while you are walking, stop and look at it while continuing to do steady breathing.

If you are walking mindfully, you should feel a sense of peace, and even happiness and joy. Continue this practice on a regular basis.

Practice Mindful Eating

Mindfulness meditation is a practice in which you try to stay in the here and now. When you have difficulty focusing, staying in the here and now can definitely be a challenge! In this worksheet, you will learn about *mindful eating*. You may have noticed that.

- Eat quickly

- Eat while doing other things, like looking at your phone

- Forget to go grocery shopping, so you grab fast food on the way home

- Go back for seconds

- Eat when you're bored or stressed

- Forget to eat meals

When you have inattention and impulsivity, you may be eating so fast that your brain may not get the signal that you are full until you are stuffed. You may also be adding on extra calories you don't burn off by not preparing healthy meals yourself. One solution to these issues is to practice "mindful eating." When you sit down to eat, just let it be you, your food, and the person with whom you are dining. This means leaving your phone, tablet, laptop, or television off. In addition, shut off the notifications on your devices.

Concentrate on what you are eating, chew slowly, and focus solely on the taste of your food. Chew at least 10 times for each bite of food. Also pay attention to where you are eating – you are more likely to eat responsibly if you are sitting down at a table rather than standing up or eating while you are walking. Make sure you are eating off a plate instead of from the box. This helps you practice portion control (how much food you are eating). Eat off a smaller plate – a study found that eating off a smaller plate helps you eat less but still feel satisfied (Van Ittersum, and Wansink, 2012).

You may start noticing that when you really focus on your food, you aren't even really enjoying what you are eating. Mindful eating sometimes makes people change what they are eating to healthier, prepared foods. Because you are eating more slowly, you may notice that you are eating less food but still feel satisfied (Daubenmier, Kristeller, Hecht, Maninger, Kuwata, and Jhaveri, et al., 2011). Practicing mindful eating even for just a few minutes at a time can be helpful. Try to increase your mindful eating time at each meal.

Practicing Deep Breathing

When we breathe, we normally practice *thoracic breathing*. This is breathing with the upper part of the chest. This is also where we breathe when we hyperventilate. When you are breathing thoracically you are not using your full lung capacity. Instead, try breathing *diaphragmatically*.

When you breathe with your diaphragm, your stomach puffs out when you inhale.

You breathe in and then up through your lungs. Then you exhale.

When you practice breathing diaphragmatically, you are using your full lung capacity.

Not only are you kicking in your parasympathetic or relaxation response, you may also be lowering your blood pressure and heart rate (Mohamed, Hanafy, and El-Naby, 2014).

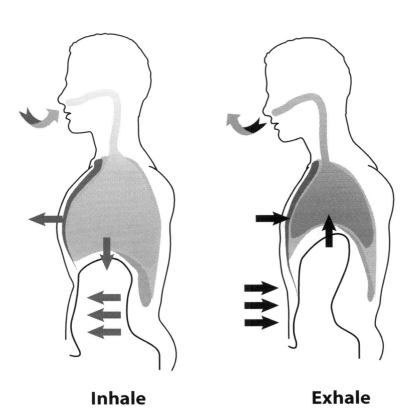

Inhale   **Exhale**

CHAPTER 6 Changing the Environment

Accommodations are ways that your client's environment can be adapted in order to help your client be efficient, productive, and work to their potential. You will learn how college accommodations are obtained and also the difference between informal versus formal accommodations in the workplace. You will also develop strategies on how help your client navigate home organization and daily functioning more easily.

Accommodations include getting all instructions from the client's employer in writing, getting a note-taker in college classes, and being able to take tests in quiet. Being able to move around during a staff meeting without penalties is also an important accommodation. As you'll learn in Chapter 8, moving around the workplace can help improve your client's ability to focus.

COLLEGE ACCOMMODATIONS

Accommodations have been shown to help people with executive dysfunction perform at the same level as their peers. Accommodations help your client get out of the "starting gate" at the same time as his classmates. Your client can apply for accommodations through his college's Office of Student Disability Services (OSDS) (or similarly named office). All public universities and any private schools that receive federal funding must provide accommodations for students with a documented disability, according to the Americans with Disabilities Act (ADA). Virtually all private universities now receive at least some federal funding like Pell Grants, so that should not be an issue.

It is recommended that students apply for accommodations as soon as they have been accepted to a college, since the approval process may take time. Colleges' websites should have a link to their OSDS offices with specific information on how to apply for accommodations.

In previous years, some colleges' OSDS offices required a full evaluation report, diagnosis, and list of recommended accommodations in order for a student to qualify for accommodations; however, the rules have changed. The focus has shifted from determining if a student has a disability to determining what type of accommodations are appropriate for the student. According to the revised Americans with Disabilities Act (ADA) and the Association for Higher Education and Disabilities (AHEAD), OSDS offices now must accept a letter from a licensed clinician stating that your client has a specific disability. You can specify in the letter the accommodations to which your client needs to gain equal access.

If your client had accommodations in high school, they should consider submitting their Section 504 or Individualized Education Plan (IEP) when applying at the OSDS. These plans already have applicable accommodations written down – and it may be more extensive than what the OSDS offers for a particular disability. Then you can also submit an addendum to these reports supporting the major accommodations that can be justified by your clinical interview and any additional assessment that you conducted. If appropriate, you can also add to the diagnosis listed on the IEP or Section 504 plan if the student has multiple disabilities.

Even if your client doesn't think they'll need a particular accommodation, consider recommending that they apply for that accommodation anyway. Clients with attention deficit hyperactivity disorder (ADHD), learning disabilities (LDs), generalized anxiety disorder (GAD), post-traumatic stress disorder (PTSD) or traumatic brain injury (TBI) may need accommodations like extended time on tests, but they are trying to avoid being seen as different than their peers. Some clients may also feel like it's "not fair" to other students that they get accommodations. Emphasize to your clients that accommodations are "equalizers" rather than "special benefits." In addition, if your client is considering going to graduate school, they must have college accommodations in place to be considered for accommodations on graduate school standardized testing such as the Medical College Admission Test (MCAT), Law School Admission Test (LSAT), Graduate Records Examinations (GRE), and Graduate Management Admission Test (GMAT).

If the OSDS doesn't approve accommodations for your client, he has the right to appeal. If your client is at a college in the U.S. and feels that the OSDS has not acted in good faith or has violated his rights, your client can contact the U.S. Office for Civil Rights. For example, a college's OSDS is not allowed to ask about a student's medication or medical treatment. For information on college accommodations and your clients' rights, see the Resources section at the end of this workbook.

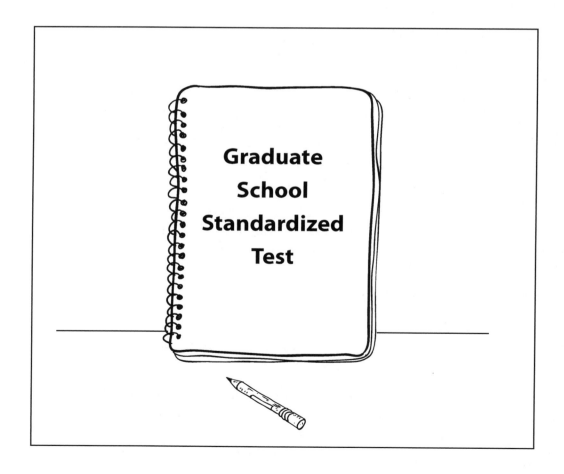

What Type of Learner Are You?

When you discover what type of learner you are, it makes your learning much more efficient. It can also help you find out what accommodations work best for you at work or at school.

For each question, select the answer that best applies to you.

- When I read something for work or school, I would rather:
    1. Read silently to myself while seated
    2. Talk about the information with someone
    3. Read out loud or silently while I walk around

- The following item is most useful to have with me while reading:
    1. A highlighter
    2. A recording of the book
    3. Something I can fiddle around with while reading

- I learn best when I:
    1. Write down key points
    2. Talk about key points
    3. Demonstrate or act out key points

- I memorize information best when I:
    1. Can look at maps and diagrams
    2. Can put the information in a rhyme or song
    3. Can act out what I've learned

- If I needed to ask someone for directions, I would remember them best if:
    1. A map was drawn for me
    2. I was told the directions
    3. The person acted out the route

If you answered mostly 1s, you are a visual learner. You would benefit from having instructions written down for you and concepts put into diagrams. You also may tend to learn better when things are color-coded.

If you answered mostly 2s, you are an auditory learner. You would benefit from audiobooks and discussing concepts with others. You also learn better from listening to lectures rather than reading.

If you answered mostly 3s, you are a kinesthetic learner. You would benefit from being able to move around while you are reading or studying. You learn better when you can "act" out concepts.

RECOMMENDED COLLEGE ACCOMMODATIONS

There are specific accommodations you may want your client to ask for if they have executive dysfunction. As you read earlier, even if your client thinks he might not use a specific accommodation, it is still recommended that the accommodation be applied for. People with executive dysfunction can have a difficult time being self-aware and realizing where they need help or where they need to make improvements. For example, college students with ADHD have more test-taking anxiety than those without ADHD (Nelson, Lindstrom, and Foels, 2014). If your client realizes late in the semester that he needs extra time on a test, he'll have that accommodation already in place. A student can use an accommodation once or whenever the need arises – they don't have to use it every single time in order to keep the accommodation.

Your client may not want to get accommodations in college due to fears that he will be "singled out" or treated differently. However, accommodations are designed to be as anonymous as possible – professors are not allowed to announce accommodations to other students, even when a student needs a note-taker in class. The college is bound by federal law to keep the client's disability information confidential – and that includes OSDS staff and professors.

Notetaker in Class

Having a notetaker in class helps your client with executive dysfunction make sure that he caught everything the professor was saying. When you are continually distracted, it can be difficult to catch everything – and if you don't write it down *right now*, that information is lost. Notetakers can either be employees of the OSDS, or a professor may ask a student at the beginning of the semester if they can be a notetaker. The student doesn't know for whom they are taking notes, nor is the professor allowed to disclose that information. The notetaker sends a copy of their notes to the professor or OSDS, who then sends the notes along to the student.

Extended Time on Tests

For many students with executive dysfunction, an hour is just not enough time to read, process, and answer all the questions on a test. Add in the distractions of someone tapping on their desk with a pencil or chairs squeaking, and it can be almost impossible to finish. If the accommodation "extended time on tests" is on your client's plan, most colleges will allow "time and a half" for tests. This means your client is allowed to take a test for the regular allotted time, plus half of that time. For example, if a test must be completed within an hour in the classroom, your client is allowed to have 1½ hours to take the test. For a student to be considered for extended time on graduate school standardized testing, such as the LSAT, MCAT, GMAT, or GRE, he must have already had extended time as an accommodation on their OSDS plan.

Testing in a Separate and Quiet Location

An accommodation of "testing in a separate and quiet location" can either mean your client is in an empty classroom with a proctor while they are taking a test, or they are taking a test in a testing center on campus with individual rooms. The former is more common on smaller campuses, while the latter is usually reserved for larger campuses. Your client must tell the professor in advance of the test if they are going to exercise their "separate and quiet location" accomodation. This is necessary in order for a testing room to be secured.

Students then do not usually attend the test being given in the classroom; instead, they appear at the testing center or empty classroom at an assigned time and date. Their test is scored the same way as it is for students who don't receive accommodations.

Ability to Record Lectures

The ability to record lectures can be accomplished through a student's phone, voice recorder, or smartpen. Without the ability to record lectures as an accommodation, professors have the right to refuse recordings. However, once it is written in your client's accommodations, he is now protected by federal law. This means your client cannot be denied the ability to record your lectures – and to do so would be a violation of federal law.

Instructions Given in Writing

For many people with executive dysfunction, merely getting verbal instructions from a professor can lead to assignments not being completed on time and not knowing there is a quiz at the next class. For many individuals with EF difficulties, it is important that they have a visual cue in order to know they have a project, assignment, or test. In addition, due to processing difficulties and issues with reconstitution of information (and executive function you learned about in Chapter 1), what your client hears and what they write down can be two different things. This is especially true if your client has ADHD, an LD, or a TBI. If your client has the accommodation of "provided with written instructions" on their plan, any project, assignment, quiz, test instruction, or announcements must be provided to your client in writing in a timely manner – whether that is through email, on the board in class, or online.

Class Syllabi Given to Student Prior to Class

Getting all syllabi from his professors prior to the first day of class gives your client the ability to plan out (with help) a study schedule ahead of time. It also means that your client knows what books they need to get prior to class. Another advantage of getting a syllabus early is being able to record all test dates into a calendar.

Use of a Smartpen

Smartpens record a professor's lecture as you write. Your client uses special paper, which then transcribes the notes onto his laptop. If your client qualifies for this accommodation, OSDS may have these pens available on site. For more information on smartpens, see the Resources section at the end of this workbook.

Priority Class Registration

Priority class registration as an accommodation means that your client gets "first dibs" on classes when registration opens. Having priority registration helps individuals with executive dysfunction in a variety of ways. First, you are more likely to get smaller class sizes. The ideal learning environment is 16 students to one instructor, so the closer your client can get to that, the better. The fewer students in class, the more likely your client will be able to pay attention and have individualized instruction. In addition, your client is more likely to ask questions in class and approach the teacher afterwards if he is in a smaller class. Secondly, many people with executive dysfunction have sleep disorders, as you will learn in Chapter 7. If your client has priority registration, they are more likely to get afternoon classes rather than 8 a.m. classes. If your client is a night owl and is able to register for afternoon classes, he is more likely to attend class and be awake and alert in class.

Third, if your client has priority registration, they are more likely to obtain "in person" classes rather than online classes. It is very important that your client go to the "in person" class. Social behavior is contagious, and being around other students who are focusing and taking notes makes it more likely that your client will do the same. In addition, as they get to know other students in class, they may be more likely to attend class. This is a phenomenon known as *social consistency*. If your client tells a friend that they will be in class on Wednesday, they are much more likely to show up. As humans, we like doing what we say we're going to do. It's a form of positive social pressure. Going to "in person" classes also mean more opportunities to form study groups. If your client knows their study group will be meeting Wednesday at 6 p.m., they are more likely to be there.

Your client is also more likely to absorb additional information from an "in person" class, and he will be more aware of information that the professor deems to be the most important. There are verbal and nonverbal cues that professors often give to let students know specific information that might be on a test – for example, "These are important points to know," or "Make sure you remember this."

Similarly, when you are in an actual class, you are able to ask questions of the professor in the moment. Otherwise, in virtual classes, you have to wait to get a response to your email or message. People with executive dysfunction need questions answered right at the time the information is given. Otherwise, they may forget the question. Professors also notice which students are asking questions, and if the professor knows your client has been working hard and involved in the class, it can make the difference between an A and a B grade.

In addition, it is highly recommended that your client goes to their professors' office hours. By asking questions, professors begin to recognize the students who are involved in the class. This ability to connect with the professor can not only help raise grades, but may also result in a recommendation letter for a job or graduate school. Reinforce to your client that professors appreciate when students come to their office hours. Some individuals with executive dysfunction, particularly those with social anxiety, can have fears about speaking with an authority figure. It is possible for you as the clinician to use video conferencing and "attend" the client's meeting with the professor. Your client is much more likely to go if you arrange a certain time or date.

Reduced Course Load

In most colleges and universities, a full course load consists of at least 12 credit hours. This usually means, at minimum, four classes of three hours a week. Sometimes, even with accommodations and hard work, students with executive dysfunction find that maintaining a full course load will lead to failing a class or classes that semester. While medical withdrawal from the semester may be an option, your client may opt to just drop a class. Sometimes that can result in students now only having six or nine credits on their schedule – which means reclassification as a part-time student. As a part-time student, students are at risk of losing their campus housing, access to services on campus, or financial aid. However, if your client has an accommodation wherein a reduced course load is counted as full-time, then they can drop down to six or nine credits and still get counted as a full-time student at the college. However, maintaining financial aid can be a challenge when students drop down to a part-time course load. It is recommended that your client and his parents speak to a financial aid representative at the college in order to try to maintain financial aid as a part-time student.

For more information on college accommodations, see the Resources section at the end of this workbook.

College Accommodations

When you have a diagnosis of attention deficit hyperactivity disorder (ADHD), a learning disability (LD), a traumatic brain injury (TBI), or other disorders characterized by executive dysfunction, you may qualify for the following accommodations at your college:

- Ability to record lectures
- Ability to have a notetaker in class
- Extended time on tests (usually time-and-a-half)
- Testing in a separate and quiet location
- Priority in class registration
- All instructions given in writing
- Use of a smartpen
- Course syllabi given prior to the first day of class

How to Apply for Accommodations

It is recommended that you apply for accommodations as soon as you have been accepted at a college.

- Go online and find the college's Office for Student Disability Services (OSDS) or similarly-named department.
- Read the instructions for applying for accommodations.
- If you had an Individualized Education Plan (IEP) or Section 504 paperwork from high school, gather this information. (If you received accommodations in school and were in speech therapy, gifted, or a class for learning disabilities, you will have an IEP. If you just received accommodations, you will have a Section 504 plan.)
- Sign a release with the college so your parents or guardian can speak to the OSDS.
- Obtain a letter from your clinician or the person who did your testing that states the name of your disorder. It is also beneficial to have a list of recommended accommodations attached to the letter.
- If you are not granted accommodations, there is a process of appeal.

For more information on college accommodations, see the National Center for College Students with Disabilities at www.nccsdonline.org.

WORKPLACE ACCOMMODATIONS

Workplace accommodations are ways in which the workplace environment can be altered in order for a client to be more productive and efficient at their job. There are two ways to seek accommodations at work – informally or formally.

Informal Workplace Accommodations

With informal accommodations, a client is getting accommodations without having to disclose his particular diagnosis to their employer. It is recommended that individuals attempt to seek informal accommodations in the workplace before proceeding with formal accommodations.

Should Your Client Tell Their Employer About their Diagnosis?

It is generally recommended that, unless your client is requesting formal accommodations through the Americans with Disabilities Act (ADA), he does not disclose his diagnosis to his employer. Unfortunately, there still remains a stigma around mental illness. This can change how your client is treated in the workplace. Additionally, third-party confidentiality cannot be guaranteed, so it is a consideration to take into account.

Formal Accommodations

If your client has attempted informal accommodations and is still not working to his potential in the workplace, your client may consider asking for formal accommodations from his employer. To be covered by the ADA in the workplace, your client must disclose his diagnosis to the appropriate party within the organization (i.e., manager, human resources department), and the diagnosis must be documented by a clinician. The ADA is a federal law that prohibits discrimination due to a disability, and it applies to businesses with 15 employees or more. If your client has a documented disability, it has been disclosed to his employer, and he is now covered under the ADA, workplace accommodations are legally binding. According to the ADA, the accommodations for which your client is asking must be reasonable – meaning that they don't go above and beyond what your workplace can reasonably do with their resources. Given that seeking formal accommodations is a time- and energy-consuming process, it is strongly recommended that your client consult with an attorney first.

If your client has disclosed his diagnosis to his employer, had his disability documented (put in writing), asked for reasonable accommodations, and still feels that his employer has not followed through with those accommodations, it is recommended that your client considers consulting with an attorney. For more information on your client's rights under the ADA, see the Resources section at the end of this workbook.

Following are some handouts and exercises to use with your client.

Workplace Accommodations
You Can Do on Your Own

Here are some accommodations you can try on your own, usually without having to talk to your boss:

- Ask for verbal instructions and requests to be sent to you in an email. This helps you keep track of assignments and requests, and it makes it less likely that you will forget to do something. It also helps you keep a "paper trail" in case a coworker or boss tells you they asked you to do something different.

- If you work in a cubicle, wear noise-cancelling headphones or earbuds to block out distracting noise.

- When scheduling your workday, allow extra time for meetings and other work events so you do not "overbook" yourself.

- Spend some time in the morning just answering emails and returning phone calls.

- Take frequent, short breaks during your workday, where you leave your desk and maybe even go outside for some fresh air.

- Go outside and take a walk during your lunch break. It is important that you get outside and move around in order to "reset" your brain.

- Break large projects into smaller tasks and assign a due date for each of these smaller tasks. You may need the help of a trusted coworker, friend, family member, or coach in order to do this.

- Make sure you receive clear deadlines, and be aware of what is expected from you.

- Shut off all notifications on your electronic devices.

- Put up a "do not disturb" sign on your cubicle or office door when you really need to focus on a project. An alternative to this is to let people know ahead of time that you need some uninterrupted time.

- Use an empty conference room or office with a door to work in when you really need to focus.

- Keep your hands busy during a meeting so you are better able to focus. This is called a "concentrated distraction." One way to do this is by using a small textured object that no one else can see as you fiddle with it.

- Continuously take notes during a meeting. This helps you stay focused and helps you better process what is going on at the meeting.

- Ask for copies of the minutes (summary) from meetings.

Role-play for Informal Accommodations

In Chapter 4, you learned about practicing role-plays with your client to better prepare them for social situations. Likewise, you can do role-plays with your client that involve asking for informal accommodations at work. Given that speaking to employers about these accommodations can be very stressful for clients, role-plays make this interaction much more tolerable.

In these role-plays, you, the clinician, are first acting as if you are the employer, and your client is playing himself or herself. Next, you both switch roles so that you are now playing the role of your client, whereas your client now assumes the role of his employer. Remember, both of you have to act "as if" – talk like you are truly that character.

The following are recommended lines for opening a dialogue with the employer:

- "Hi Mr. Employer, I was wondering if I could talk to you about some ideas I have to help my productivity."
- "Hi Mr. Employer, I'd like to schedule some time to meet with you."
- "Hi Mr. Employer, do you have a few minutes?"

As your client practices role-plays such as these, he will become much more comfortable in that environment. Encourage your client to practice these role-plays at home. Be aware that the client may be more successful if they frame these requests as a means by which to be more productive and efficient in the workplace. It is recommended that your client asks the employer for only two or three accommodations at a time. Remember that when asking for informal accommodations, your client doesn't mention his diagnosis.

ADA Formal Accommodations for the Workplace

The Americans with Disabilities Act (ADA) is a federal act that protects people with disabilities in the workplace. Accommodations you can ask your employer for include:

- Having a weekly one-on-one meeting with your boss to review assignments, projects, and your performance.

- Getting an assistant to help you complete detailed paperwork and to take phone calls.

- Moving your office out of the main working area in order to decrease distractions. An ideal office for you is at the end of the hall.

- Getting an office with a door instead of working in a cubicle.

- Being allowed to stand up during meetings.

- Getting flexible work hours. If you come in at 8 a.m. and leave at 4 a.m., or get in at 10 a.m. and leave at 6 p.m., you are not only beating traffic, you are also giving yourself some time in the office by yourself, when there will be fewer distractions.

HOME ACCOMMODATIONS

Home life can be very challenging for people with executive dysfunction. There are expectations of organization, productivity, and money management, to name just a few.

Here are some ways that you can help your client have a happier and more productive home life.

Reduce Visual Stress

Clutter creates *visual stress*, a feeling of overload when you see all the stacks of papers on the counter and things in disarray. While eliminating clutter is ideal, it is not always realistic. Covering up clutter is a quick way to reduce visual stress. It can help your client feel more comfortable about having people over to his house. Have an empty trunk or a piece of furniture that doubles as storage space. If company comes over unexpectedly, your client can dump the clutter into the trunk. (If a few months have passed and your client hasn't needed to get any of the papers out, consider throwing them out.) In addition, choose wall units and other items of furniture that have built-in doors that can be closed when your client is not using the items inside. Just by shutting doors on wall units and shelves, your client immediately reduces the amount of visual stress in his home. Your client will feel less overwhelmed when his clutter "disappears."

Use GPS Trackers on Frequently Lost Items

It can be really difficult to keep track of smaller items, like a cell phone or keys. One way to keep track of these items is to attach a GPS tracker. These trackers stick onto items or can be attached to a key chain. A phone or computer app tracks the items' location. A GPS tracker can even be attached to a dog's collar. Have your client consider getting a keychain that lists a P.O. Box so people can mail keys back to you. For more information on trackers, please see the Resources section at the end of this chapter.

Use a Digital Lock Instead of Keys

One way to avoid losing house keys is to not need them anymore. There are several door locks available where you punch in a code to your keypad instead of using a key. The code can be changed by the home owner at any time. There are some digital locks that also combine a key lock. The key lock can override the digital lock in case your client forgets the door code.

Household Accommodations

Having issues with organizing, prioritizing, and time management can cause a lot of stress for you at home. Here are some tips to make your home life easier.

HAVE A "DUMPING" STATION NEAR YOUR FRONT DOOR

Have a tray near your front door where you drop your keys, wallet, and phone when you get home from work. This increases your chances of finding those items when you go to work the next morning.

USE THE POINT OF PERFORMANCE

You may lose your keys frequently or you may realize in the grocery store checkout that you've forgotten your wallet. Losing items can be common when you have executive function challenges. One way to keep track of your items is to keep them at the *point of performance* – where you are most likely to look for them and use them. For example, your keys and wallet should be placed in a small basket by the front door. When you get home, put your keys and wallet in the basket right away.

USE NOTES

Before you leave the house, check yourself to make sure you have the *trifecta* – your phone, wallet, and keys. Even put a sign up by your front door that says

---

Do You Have Your
Wallet ☑   **Keys** ☑   **Phone** ☑

If you have difficulty remembering to brush and floss your teeth before bed, make a list of your bathroom tasks and stick it to your bathroom mirror. You can also use dry erase markers to write on your mirror.

GET CLEAR BINS – IN YOUR REFRIGERATOR AND ELSEWHERE

When you have executive dysfunction, you have to see things to know they exist. When storing items in containers, get clear ones with locking handles. It is very helpful to see what is inside the container instead of guessing. A secure lid means that if you accidentally tip it over, nothing spills out. You can even get clear drawers for your refrigerator. Stop making your vegetable crisper drawer into a vegetable rotter drawer.

USE A ROLLING CART TO PUT THINGS AWAY

Get a rolling laundry cart with three or four compartments, one for each room in your house. As you go through the house, take items that belong in different rooms and put them in their respective compartment in the cart. As you move to the next room, put back the items from the cart, and put in new ones that need to be relocated. This makes cleanup much more efficient.

GET AUTO-SHUTOFF APPLIANCES

Sometimes people who are distracted leave their kitchen appliances on when they leave the house. This can have disastrous consequences. Make sure when you buy appliances that they have an auto-shutoff feature – and make sure that feature is engaged (on). Even stovetops and ovens have auto-shutoff features. Some digital household assistants or "smart homes" can turn off appliances, even when you are at work.

AVOID USING CANDLES

If you have difficulties with distraction and forgetfulness, stay away from using candles in your home. People who are distracted can tend to forget to blow candles out, greatly increasing the risk for a fire. There are many varieties of "battery-powered candles" that look very similar to the real thing.

USE TIMERS

Using timers and calendar notifications helps you stay on track with your schedule. Luckily, in the age of smartphones, you can set multiple timers at once.

Set your timers for:

- Taking medication

- When you are supposed to pick up your kids from school

- When you have a meeting

- When you are supposed to leave the house

PICK UP FOR 15 MINUTES EACH NIGHT

Before you go to bed, set a timer for 15 minutes. Pick up as much as you can until the timer goes off. When you pick up in small increments it makes a big difference.

LEAVE EVERY ROOM CLEANER THAN WHEN YOU ENTERED IT

Whenever you go into a room, find something to pick up, even if it's a small bit of paper on the floor. Over time you will notice your living space is much cleaner. It also will take you less time to do deep cleaning in the future.

Sort Through Items on a Regular Basis

The simpler the decluttering process is, the easier it will be to follow through. To begin, get four large boxes, one large garbage bag, and a permanent marker. Sort through at least 10 items a day. To make this process less stressful, do it for no more than 30 minutes a day. Set a timer before you begin. It also helps to have a trusted friend, family member, coach, or organizer with you when you sort through your stuff.

- **Label the first box "Fix It."** Put items in this box that are not working properly and are repairable. Before putting an item in this box, ask yourself if repairing the item is worth your time and money.

- **Label the second box "Give It Away."** This box is for items that would be enjoyed or used more by a charitable organization or by your family or friends.

- **Label the third box "Keep It."** This box is for items that are in good working order and have been used in the past year. This box is also for items that have sentimental value.

- **Label the fourth box "Don't Know."** Use this box if you are unsure whether or not you need an item. Put this box away for a year. If you did not use the item during that time, you probably do not need it.

- **The fifth "box" is your garbage bag.** The garbage bag is for items that are broken and are not repairable or items that do not have value to you or anyone else. When the bag is full, put it in your trash can.

Sort through your belongings and put them in the appropriate box. Try to categorize the items as quickly but as thoughtfully as possible. The longer you hold on to an item, the harder it is to let it go. Consider having a trusted friend or family member help you with the sorting process. It is recommended you sort for 30 minutes with a 15 minute-break.

CHAPTER 7 Practicing Good Self-Care

In this chapter, you'll learn how sleep and diet can impact your client's wellbeing and executive function (EF) performance. There will be tips on how to get your client assessed for sleep disorders, help him stay on a more even keel emotionally, and help him come out of the common spiral of guilt and shame that often accompanies executive dysfunction. You will also discover why people with executive dysfunction are more likely to have eating disorders and what you can do about it.

SLEEP

People with EF difficulties often experience:

- Early insomnia (difficulties falling asleep)
- Middle insomnia (waking up in the middle of the night)
- Terminal insomnia (waking up too early and not being able to get back to sleep)
- Obstructive sleep apnea
- Restless leg syndrome
- Snoring
- Moving around a lot while sleeping
- Confusional arousals (the body is awake, but the brain is still asleep)

(Silvestri et al., 2009)

When your clients are sleep deprived, they have even more difficulties concentrating and focusing, have a slower brain processing speed, and have more difficulties with executive function skills, like working memory (Blesch and McCoy, 2013; Goel et al., 2009). They are even more likely to abuse substances if they are sleep deprived (McKnight-Eily, Eaton, Lowry, Croft, Presley-Cantrell, and Perry, 2011). Sleep disorders become a vicious cycle for people with executive function difficulties.

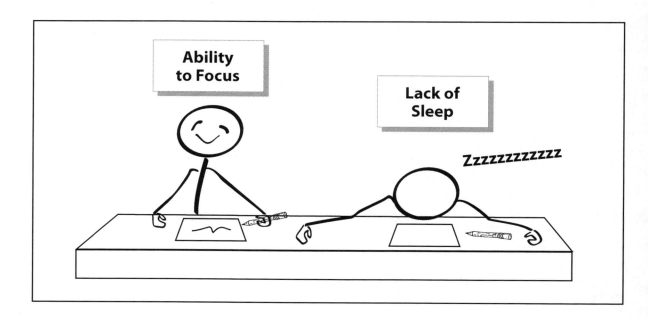

Genetics

There is a strong association between genes and sleep disorders. Individuals with variations in a genetic marker have been found to exhibit significantly decreased performance on both EF and non-EF tasks when they were sleep-deprived, and this performance worsened during the night (Groeger, Viola, Lo, von Schantz, Archer, and Dijk, 2008).

Obstructive Sleep Apnea

Obstructive sleep apnea (OSA) is a serious sleep disorder that can exacerbate already existing difficulties with EF performance (Youssef, Ege, Angly, Strauss, and Marx, 2011; Beebe, 2005). During an OSA episode, the soft tissue in the back of the throat blocks a person's airway. They don't awaken fully, but breathing is interrupted. Your client can't reach the rapid eye movement (REM) deep level of sleep when this occurs.

Common symptoms of OSA include:

- Snoring
- Waking up still feeling fatigued
- Moving around a lot while sleeping
- Breathing through the mouth
- Making choking or snorting sounds while sleeping
- Spouse/partner waking up because the sleeper has stopped breathing
- Waking up during the night

(Fisher, 2013)

A client is more likely to have sleep apnea if he:

- Has ADHD
- Is overweight or obese
- Has a neck girth of 17 inches or more
- Has a family history of sleep apnea

If your client has sleep apnea, there is a 95% chance that he has additional problems paying attention and focusing on top of his already existing EF issues (Youssef et al., 2011). If your client has ADHD in particular, there's a 20-30% chance they also have sleep apnea (Youssef et al., 2011).

Untreated sleep apnea can lead to:

- Increased risk of heart attack
- Increased risk of stroke
- Difficulties losing weight
- Relationship issues (due to snoring)
- Early death

Sleep disorders are best diagnosed in a sleep lab, including getting an accurate diagnosis of sleep apnea (Fisher, 2013). Sleep labs are either "stand alone" labs or they are connected to hospitals. A sleep lab does more than just assess for sleep apnea – they also test for other sleep disorders, like restless leg syndrome and seizures.

The treatment for sleep apnea involves a continuous positive airway pressure machine (CPAP), which is a breathing appliance used at night. It's the size of a small box and has tubing with a mask or nasal pillows attached. When your client wears a CPAP, it gives a continuous flow of air pressure to keep the throat passages open at night. When you see your client after CPAP treatment, you may notice a complete difference in alertness, attitude, and even quite a bit of weight loss. Deep rapid eye movement sleep (REM) is where we burn off our fat stores and heal ourselves – and with sleep apnea, people are not reaching that deep level of sleep.

Next you will find a worksheet for determining the level of sleep deprivation in your client.

Writing a Prescription for a Sleep Lab

To be seen at a sleep lab, a person must have a referral from a clinician. The following form should be enough data to get your client admitted to a lab.

Name: _____ Date of Birth: _____

Date:_____

Length and nature of current treatment with this clinician:

Symptoms of sleep disorders:

Length of time symptoms have occurred:

Current diagnosis and medication:

_____

Clinician Signature   Date

Getting Ready for a Sleep Study

Your doctor has referred you for a sleep study. Congratulations! You are among the handful of people who get to experience one of the most interesting medical tests ever. Your visit to the sleep lab will give your doctor valuable information that can help you have a better quality of life.

WHAT TO EXPECT

You will check into the sleep lab in the late afternoon. Your room will look like a regular hotel room, except with an infrared camera and a PA speaker. This allows the sleep lab staff to watch you sleeping and also allows you to talk with them back and forth. You will be fitted with:

- A respirator band that fits around your chest, in order to check for breathing interruptions

- Electroencephalogram (EEG) leads – stickers that are attached to your head, in order to measure your brain waves and to check if you are having a seizure while you sleep (a rare occurrence)

- Electrocardiogram (EKG) leads – stickers that are attached to your chest, arms and legs, to measure if your heart is working okay

- Restless leg leads – stickers attached to your legs to measure if your legs are overactive while you sleep

Your job while you are at the sleep lab is to… sleep. That's it. The sleep lab will take care of the rest. Some people report being at the sleep lab was one of the most restful nights of sleep they have had in a long time.

If you have any questions while you are at the sleep lab, just speak up – the staff will be able to hear you over the speaker system. Good luck, and good sleeping!

Turn Off Electronics At Least Two Hours Before Bed

Melatonin is a brain chemical (or hormone) that helps you fall asleep. Your brain releases melatonin to help it get ready for sleep. People with executive function difficulties, especially ADHD, already may have difficulties getting melatonin released in their brains in time to fall asleep at a reasonable hour.

When you use backlit electronic devices in the two hours before you go to bed, you are more likely to have insomnia and increased difficulties getting up in the morning (Fossum, Nordnes, Storemark, Bjorvatn, and Pallesen, 2014). Backlit devices give off a wavelength of light that mimics sunlight, which decreases melatonin production in the brain (Wood, Rea, Plitick, and Figueiro, 2013).

Backlit devices include:

- Smartphones

- Laptops

- Desktop monitors

- Televisions

- Tablets

Engage in a relaxing activity before bed. This provides a good transition from your busy day into restful sleep.

Practicing Good Sleep Habits

If your client has EF difficulties, the chances are that he also has a sleep disorder and may not be practicing the best sleep habits. The following are some sleep issues to consider when meeting with your client.

People Need At Least 8 Hours of Sleep a Night

For the average adult, seven to nine hours of sleep is essential for brain and body health, not to mention emotional health – with children needing even more to ensure proper growth and development (Hirshkowitz et al., 2015). When individuals get less sleep than is recommended, the chance that they will develop health issues increases. Chronic sleep deprivation can lead to increased chances of substance abuse, depression, and a shortened life span (Centers for Disease Control and Prevention, 2011; McKnight-Elly, Eaton, Lowry, Croft, Presley-Cantrell, and Perry, 2011).

Being Aware of a Body Clock

Many people with executive function difficulties do not keep a "standard" sleep pattern – if they could make their own sleep/wake hours, they would go to bed around 4 a.m. and get up at 1 p.m. Some brains just work better in evening hours. Instead of fighting that fact, you and your client can look into finding a job where he can work a night shift. Similarly, look into careers for your client that have flexible work hours where your client will not be penalized if he shows up at 10 a.m. and works until 6 p.m., rather than the standard 9 a.m. to 5 p.m.

Coming in later and leaving later often works better for individuals with executive dysfunction for various reasons. One of these reasons is that they are more likely to avoid traffic – a nightmare for people with executive dysfunction, due to frustration and impulsivity. In addition, forcing a brain to work early morning hours when it is just not wired to do so produces even more workplace difficulties than are already inherent among people with executive dysfunction. In order to determine if your client is a "night owl," ask what work hours your client would want to have if he could make his own schedule without penalty.

Keep in mind that sleep patterns can also have a genetic influence – ask if either of your client's parents or any siblings tend to stay up late or prefer to wake up early.

Careers for Night Owls

You may prefer to go to bed in the early hours of the morning and sleep in late. Being a night owl is genetic in many cases – there is a chance that at least one of your parents is also a night owl. If being alert and getting to work on time in the morning is a challenge, consider a career where you can have night hours. Having a job that works with your body clock may lead to less sleep deprivation and better focus.

CAREERS WHERE NIGHT HOURS MIGHT BE AVAILABLE INCLUDE:

- Paramedic
- Emergency medical technician
- Sleep lab staff
- Information technology staff
- Medical sonographer
- Hotel night auditor
- Residential counselor
- Crisis center staff
- Certified nursing assistant
- Home health aide
- Emergency room physician
- Emergency room nurse
- Emergency room technician
- ICU nurse
- Surgical floor nurse
- Security guard
- Law enforcement officer

- Editor
- Hotel desk staff
- Driver
- Power plant staff
- Doorman
- Freelance writer
- Mail sorter
- Customer service representative
- Online moderator
- Physicians assistant
- Firefighter
- Restaurant server
- Third-shift factory worker
- Airport baggage handler
- Baker
- Software coder
- Construction

Good Sleep Hygiene Tips

- Keep the Same Wake and Bed Times Every Day
  - Your body can't compensate for staying up late on weekends.

- Have a Completely Dark Room
  - Consider getting curtains that block out sunlight.

- Use Background Sound
  - Have relaxing music or a guided imagery recording.

- Keep Your Bedroom Clutter-Free
  - Spend 15 minutes before bed picking up.

- Only Use Your Bed for Sleep and Sex
  - Don't do work, read, or eat in bed, as your brain will associate your bed with factors other than sleep, including stress.

- Shut Off Backlit Devices an Hour Before Bed
  - Studies have found this helps you fall asleep more easily.

- Get Enough Sleep
  - You need at least seven to nine hours of sleep per night.

- Get a Sleep Lab Study
  - A study can help determine if you have sleep apnea, restless leg, and/or other sleep disorders. See your doctor.

- Avoid Caffeine Before Bed
  - Caffeine is a stimulant and can keep you awake.

- Practice Journaling
  - Write your concerns and worries out before bed, along with a list of things that went well that day.

Keep a Sleep Diary

Write down (or voice record) when you go to bed each night, and when you get up in the morning. Also record:

- What time you took your medication that day (or evening).

- What time you started getting ready for bed.

- How much alcohol, if any, you drank that evening.

- The temperature of the room.

- The darkness of the room.

- Your general health that day.

- Your current stress level.

- If you engaged in a relaxing activity before bed, or if you were using electronics up until you went to sleep.

- What time you got in bed.

- How long it took you to go to sleep.

- If you woke up in the middle of the night and how long it took you to go back to sleep.

Just keeping track of your sleep habits can help you adjust your behavior so you are more likely to get a good night's rest (Kira, Maddison, Hull, Blunden, and Olds, 2014). Take this "sleep log" to your doctor if you are continuing to have problems getting a good night's rest.

There are also apps that can help you track your sleep habits. Some apps are in a journal format, while others have you put your phone on the bed while you sleep, in order to track movement.

DIET

Food is medicine for the body. The adage "you are what you eat" really is true. Individuals with executive dysfunction can have a complicated relationship with food. As you will read in this section, EF difficulties can lead to eating disorders and forgetting to eat regularly. Before starting any diet plan, clients should check with their doctor. In Chapter 5, you learned about a mindful eating practice. In this section, you will learn even more about the importance of your clients with executive dysfunction learning healthy eating behaviors.

EATING DISORDERS AND EXECUTIVE FUNCTION

Individuals with obesity and anorexia nervosa have been found to demonstrate impaired performance on measures of executive functioning compared to healthy weight individuals, with obese individuals in particular exhibiting the greatest difficulties on inhibition tasks (Fagundo et al., 2012). Another study found that individuals who are obese and engage in binge eating exhibit greater impairments on measures of problem-solving, cognitive flexibility, and working memory compared to people with obesity who do not engage in binge eating (Monica et al., 2010).

The rate of eating disorders among individuals with ADHD is four times higher than the general population, as they are more likely to overeat, and be overweight or obese than those without ADHD (Cortese and Vincenzi, 2012; Davis, 2010; Pagoto et al., 2009; Strimas et al., 2008). Is it that EF difficulties lead to the development of eating disorders, or do eating disorders lead to EF difficulties? It is unclear at this point, but research favors the view that executive dysfunction, in part, leads to development of eating disorders. This is particularly the case when you look at the role of impulsivity and lack of inhibition in executive dysfunction.

WHAT IS A HEALTHY DIET?

A healthy diet is one that is low in unhealthy fats, high in quality protein, high in carbohydrates, high in fatty acids, and high in mineral content (Woo et al., 2014). People with ADHD tend to have poorer nutrition and take in more calories than people without ADHD (van Egmond-Fröhlich, Weghuber, and de Zwaan, 2012). Food can be a form of self-medication for people with executive dysfunction. When you eat a food that is high in sugar, salt, or fat, it triggers a brain reaction that is the same as if you were abusing drugs (Davis, 2010).

Is Your Client Experiencing an Eating Disorder?

Because eating disorders are more common among individuals with executive function, here's a checklist to help determine if it is an issue for your client.

- ❑ Excessive weight loss or gain over the last six months

- ❑ Perfectionistic tendencies

- ❑ Bruised or callused knuckles or fingers

- ❑ Loss of hair

- ❑ Hoarding food

- ❑ Secretive eating

- ❑ Making large quantities of high-fat foods for others

- ❑ Gaunt appearance

- ❑ History of vomiting

- ❑ Use of laxatives

- ❑ Excessive use of mirrors

If your client meets even one of these criteria, ask further to determine if your client might meet the diagnostic criteria for anorexic disorder, bulimic disorder, or binge eating disorder.

Keeping Track of What You Eat

Writing down what you eat during the day can reduce your chances of overeating. It can also help you figure out where you need to cut back on your food intake – or if you need to eat more. **Warning:** If you have a history of anorexia nervosa, it is not recommended that you track your food intake, as it may trigger relapse.

	Sunday	Monday	Tuesday	Wednesday	Thursday	Friday	Saturday
Breakfast							
Lunch							
Dinner							
Snacks							

Tips for Healthy Eating

Try the following tips for healthier eating – it can lead to better overall wellbeing.

- Reduce use of refined sugars

- Cut out trans fats

- Increase consumption of water

- Decrease consumption of sodas, including diet sodas

- Limit drinking high-sugar fruit juices

- Eat more fresh food and less processed food

- Practice mindful eating

- Learn proper portion sizes and practice portion control

- Avoid skipping meals

- Eat several smaller meals during the day rather than three larger meals

- Do not eat off anyone's plate, including your kid's plate

- Avoid fad diets

Become Aware of Your Body's Signals

Sometimes when people have executive function issues, they have difficulty paying attention to how their body is feeling. There are so many distractions and things you have to get done! You may also hyperfocus and forget to eat. Your body gives you "cues" or signals that it is hungry or thirsty. Practice mindfulness during the day to check in with yourself to see if you need to eat or drink. Stop what you are doing, and check in with yourself. What is your body telling you? Signs of hunger and thirst include:

- Growling stomach
- Feeling lightheaded
- Dry mouth
- Shaking hands
- Extremities (hands and feet) feel cold
- Mood changes (especially increased irritability)

To prevent yourself from not eating enough, try the following:

- Set a timer on your phone to remind you when to eat
- Carry a high-protein snack with you
- Keep high-protein snacks and bottled water in your car and in your desk at work

Portable and nonperishable high-protein snacks include:

- Nuts
- Beef or turkey jerky
- Protein bar
- Pumpkin seeds or sesame seeds
- Roasted chickpeas
- Pre-prepared hummus and chips

REGULATING EMOTIONS

As you learned in Chapter 1, one of the EFs involves the ability to regulate emotions. When people have emotion regulation issues, they have difficulty staying on an "even keel." They tend to experience mood lability, to differing degrees. It is also difficult for people with executive dysfunction to realize when they are getting too frustrated or keyed up.

TAKING BREAKS

When people with executive dysfunction focus on a task, they tend to get laser-sharp focus, or *hyperfocus*. Someone could be calling their name, their phone may be ringing – and they don't hear it. When you ask them how much time they have spent on an enjoyable task, they grossly underestimate the length of time. Some people with executive dysfunction may forget to eat or even go to the bathroom when they are in this hyperfocused state. As you learned earlier in this workbook, executive dysfunction doesn't only involve problems with attention – it also involves problems with motivation. The brain has difficulty motivating itself to pay attention to things by which it is not excited and has difficulty tearing itself away from things it really likes. The detriment of this is that the person with executive dysfunction can get burned out very easily after these periods of intense focus.

It is important that breaks are scheduled into your client's day, even if he wants to keep working. It is recommended that your client sets a timer for 30 minutes, then takes a 15-minute break, works for another 30 minutes, and then takes another 15-minute break. During these breaks, it is important that your client gets up and moves around – preferably by going outside. As you'll see in the next chapter, movement and being outside are two of the most effective non-medication treatments for executive dysfunction.

Pay Attention to How Your Body Feels When you are Angry

When you have EF difficulties, sometimes you get angry easily. Your emotions show up without much warning. Identifying how your body feels when anger is ramping up can help you use that energy in a more positive way.

Using the drawing below, write next to each part of the body how it feels when you get upset:

What feelings does your body experience first when you get upset?

_____

_____

_____

_____

Focus on your breathing and how you feel the next time you start feeling these emotions come on. What could you do to help yourself stay calm?

_____

_____

_____

_____

Setting Up a Work/Break Schedule

When you have difficulties with executive function, you may find yourself distracted at certain times and then *too* focused on something at other times. That's because your frontal lobes not only contribute to problems with paying attention, they also contribute to difficulties in getting motivated. When you really like something, you can have laser-sharp focus – to the point where you forget to eat or even go to the bathroom and sleep. When you are able to focus like this, your brain can get tired and you can get burned out. You'll know you are burned out when:

- You feel like you don't really have a purpose in life
- Things feel like they are the same all the time
- You don't really enjoy the things you used to

It's very important to take regular breaks when you are working, even if your brain says "go, go, go!" Follow the schedule below to make sure you are giving your brain and body a break.

Before starting a project or activity:

- Set your phone timer for 30 minutes
- When the timer goes off, set it for 15 minutes
- Take a 15-minute break
- Go outside and move around (this helps reset your brain)
- Have someone "kick you back into play" if you aren't going back in after 15 minutes
- Repeat

The more you give yourself scheduled breaks, the more your brain will thank you! You will also find you actually get more work done in the long run.

TIPS

Giving Your Client
Permission to Let Go

It is important that clients are able to identify the guilt and shame spiral to which they may have become accustomed due to difficulties with their impulsivity or distractibility. Likewise, it is important to teach your clients about the importance of forgiving themselves. As the saying goes, "Forgiveness is giving up the hope that the past could be any different." Sometimes clients have issues with anger or frustration because they are actually upset with themselves, not with the world around them. It is important to emphasize that there are some things in life over which we do not have control (see an exercise about this in the CBT chapter, Chapter 4). Sometimes we as clinicians need to literally give clients permission to let go of the past.

Ways to help your client let go of past shame and guilt include:

- Using an empty chair technique where your client talks to their inner self or a person who has hurt them.

- Writing a letter to themselves or to a person who has hurt them, and then destroying the letter.

- Having the client visualize an event in their life that caused them guilt and shame and having them turn this visualization into a black and white image, around which they visualize putting a frame, hanging it on the wall, and walking away from it.

Emphasize to your client that forgiveness is a multistep process, and even doing a little at a time still counts.

CHAPTER 8 Movement and Exercise

Exercise increases levels of the neurotransmitters dopamine, serotonin, norepinephrine, and gamma-Aminobutyric acid (GABA) (Rommel, Halperin, Asherson, and Kuntsi, 2013; Archer and Kostrzewa, 2012; Durston, 2010; Kiluk, Weden, and Culotta, 2009). Even exercising once can improve executive function performance (MacIntosh et al., 2014). Indeed, 5 to 30 minutes of exercise has been found to help improve executive function (EF) performance in children with ADHD (Grassmann, Alves, Santos-Galduróz, and Galduróz, 2014; Gawrilow, Stadler, Langguth, Nauman, and Boeck, 2013). Other studies have found that exercising for 20 minutes helps raise low neurotransmitter levels, whereas 30 minutes of exercise results in improved performance on an executive function and EF performance test (Wigal, Emmerson, Gehricke, and Galassetti, 2013). Exercise has also been found to decrease levels of depression and anxiety (Jonsdottir, Gerber, Lindwall, Lindegård, and Börjesson, 2013).

Not only can exercise improve executive function performance, but it can also lead to improvements in social skills, motor coordination, and strength (Kamp, Sperlich, and Holmberg, 2014). When discussing exercise with clients, consider reframing it as "fitness" instead. The word "exercise" has negative connotations for many.

RECOMMENDED AMOUNTS OF EXERCISE

Although the U.S. Department of Health and Human Services recommends one hour or more of physical activity every day, it is estimated that only 40% of people in the U.S. get this recommended amount of exercise (U.S. Department of Health and Human Services, 2012). This percentage is thought to be even lower among individuals with executive dysfunction, as they exhibit deficits in regions of the brain associated with motivation.

YOGA AND MARTIAL ARTS

Consider recommending yoga and/or martial arts to clients with EF difficulties, as several studies have found that martial arts are beneficial to EF performance (Marquez-Castillo, 2013; Sánchez-López, Fernández, Silva-Pereyra, and Martínez Mesa, 2013; Lakes and Hoyt, 2004). Tai chi, a form of martial arts, can help improve EF performance, including mood regulation, with evidence that tai chi has some lasting effects on EF after training is completed (Converse, Ahlers, Travers, and Davidson, 2014; Caldwell et al., 2011). Tai chi also has been shown to reduce the level of cortisol, a stress-related hormone, in the body and may even improve the way the immune system functions (Wang and An, 2011; Esch et al., 2007).

People with EF difficulties who have practiced martial arts have stated that their brain has learned to self-regulate automatically as a result of practicing martial arts. In addition, martial arts are taught in increments of information called *katas*. Learning in increments of information is helpful to individuals with executive dysfunction, as information is processed more easily and more effectively when it is broken down into smaller pieces.

Practicing yoga regularly may also help reduce the severity of ADHD symptoms, including hyperactivity, impulsivity, mild mood swings, depression, and anxiety (Hariprasad, Arasappa, Varambally, Srinath, and Gangadhar, 2013; Streeter et al., 2010; Haffner, Roos, Goldstein, Parzer, and Resch, 2006; Jensen and Kenny, 2004). A review of 81 studies found that yoga helped reduce fatigue, pain, blood glucose levels (associated with diabetes), blood lipids (associated with cholesterol), and sleep difficulties (Ross and Thomas, 2010). It also helped reduce the amount of cortisol, a stress-produced hormone, in the body.

Yoga and martial arts are easily accessible and are relatively low-cost. They also, in part, focus on diaphragmatic breathing combined with movement, which is an important skill for people with executive dysfunction to employ in order to decrease stress (Mohamed, Hanafy, and El-Naby, 2014). There is a diaphragmatic breathing exercise worksheet for your client in Chapter 5.

The following handouts and worksheets are tools you can give clients to promote exercise and activity:

- Yoga Poses for Focus and Attention
- Be Active at Work
- Types of Exercise
- Ways I Can Get Exercise

Yoga Poses for Focus and Attention

Whether yoga is new to you or you have been doing it for quite a while, the following are poses that most people can master right away. These poses are thought to help people with attention and focus. Remember to work at your own pace, and always check with your doctor before starting an exercise program.

STANDING POSES

MOUNTAIN POSE

WARRIOR 2

TREE POSE

**STANDING
FORWARD BEND**

SEATED POSES

**SEATED
FORWARD BEND**

**THUNDERBOLT
POSE**

**SEATED
MOUNTAIN
POSE**

Be Active at Work

When an individual has executive dysfunction, sitting at a desk all day at work is like torture. Individuals with executive function difficulties need to move around while they work. When you move around, you are stimulating a part of the brain called the *cerebellum*. This part of the brain helps with movement and balance. When your cerebellum is stimulated, your frontal lobes – the home of the executive functions – are better able to focus. This process of moving to help you focus is called *concentrated distraction*. There is also an added benefit to moving while you are at work - if you are active before and after learning something new, your brain is more likely to hold on to that information (Mavilidi, Okely, Chandler, and Paas, 2016).

Here are ways to incorporate movement into your workday:

- Sit on a large stability ball while you're at your desk, or get a chair that incorporates a stability ball.

- Sit on a chair that requires movement and balance in order to stay seated.

- Use a "stand-up" desk. There are desks that can be moved to a standing position with the press of a button.

- Get bicycle pedals that fit under the desk. These are not visible to someone walking by, and they are silent.

- Walk outside during breaks. Movement and being outside help "reset" the brain.

- Take regular breaks to walk to the restroom.

Additional tips:

- Take the stairs instead of the elevator.

- Park further away from the office.

- Take a walk during lunch hour.

- Have a "fidget" object that can be fiddled with while working.

- Stand up in the back of the room during meetings, if possible.

- Find a job that incorporates movement as part of the workday.

Types of Exercise

The U.S. Department of Health and Human Services (2012) advises that daily exercise should be a combination of mostly aerobic activity of moderate or vigorous intensity (at least breaking a light sweat), as well as muscle- and bone-strengthening exercises.

- **AEROBIC ACTIVITY**

    Aerobic exercises increase heart rate and the amount of oxygen a person uses. Examples of aerobic activities include jogging, swimming, cycling, and walking.

- **MUSCLE-STRENGTHENING**

    Muscle-strengthening exercises are those where the body, weights, or other resistance is moved against gravity (National Osteoporosis Foundation, 2014). Muscle-strengthening exercises include lifting weights, using exercise bands, and doing push-ups.

- **BONE-STRENGTHENING**

    Bone-strengthening exercises are ones in which a person stays upright and moves against gravity (National Osteoporosis Foundation, 2014). Bone-strengthening exercises include jumping rope, tennis, and fast walking.

How to Begin a Fitness Program

If exercise hasn't been part of your daily routine, getting started can be a challenge. Here are some guidelines to help you.

- Have a varied exercise plan to keep up your interest.

- Do activities that are within your ability level. Overexertion can lead to sports injuries.

- Find an exercise partner. You are more likely to stick with a fitness program if you have another person motivating you. There are apps and websites that can match you up with people by location, ability level, schedule, and preferred activities.

- Exercise first thing in the morning to get the maximum benefits of increased brain chemicals.

- Start low and go slow. Even exercising for 20 minutes helps raise brain chemical levels, and 30 minutes of exercise improves your brain's executive functions.

- Talk to your doctor before starting any fitness program.

TIPS

Help Your Client Create an Exercise Program

People with executive dysfunction tend to like exercise programs where there is/are:

- Variety
- Social contact
- Structure (a class that meets every Wednesday night at 6 p.m.)
- No "right" way to do the exercise (proper form is not emphasized)
- Limited or no rules to the exercise
- No need to keep score
- No special equipment needed
- Easy-to-do movements
- A limited amount of time to exercise
- An instructor who gives positive feedback
- A reward system (points you earn per activity)

Simplicity and accessibility is key. People with EF difficulties tend to like the following forms of exercise, both recreationally and competitively:

- Swimming
- Walking
- Running
- Dancing
- Cycling
- Martial Arts
- Yoga

Ways I Can Get Exercise

Look for ways you can sneak exercise into your day. Taking the stairs instead of the elevator counts! Take a moment to write down ways you like to be active. The best types of exercise are ones that can be done anywhere, don't need any extra equipment, don't require spending any money, and don't require anyone teaching you how to do it. Walking around the block, for example, fits all those descriptions.

Activity	Where	When

THE IMPORTANCE OF BEING OUTSIDE

Studies have found that being outside while being active can help improve executive dysfunction. For example, a study by Taylor and Kuo (2009) found that children with ADHD exhibited a greater reduction of symptoms when they were allowed to be active outside instead of staying in the classroom. People with EF difficulties will describe their time outside as "resetting" their brains. They also have described the sensation as their "brain slowing down to match the pace of nature." When people are engaged in "play" outside, their voluntary attention turns off and their involuntary attention kicks in.

Voluntary attention is the focus you use to read something at work – you make a concentrated effort to absorb the material. This voluntary attention is an area where individuals with executive dysfunction expend a lot of energy – and it makes their brains very tired. Involuntary attention is what your brain does when you are just enjoying yourself and are not focused on any outcomes. In other words, turning on involuntary attention helps your brain rest for a while. As you read earlier in the chapter, it is important that people with executive dysfunction take a walk outside during their work breaks; even exercising for 15 to 20 minutes can help improve executive function performance.

CHAPTER 9 Day-to-Day Living

In this chapter, you will learn about the day-to-day issues facing people with executive dysfunction. Issues with careers, relationships, money, and addiction are all too common. Discover tips on how to help your client find a job that is best suited to his needs. You will also learn how to help your client set boundaries, establish healthy relationships, and manage spending money. You will also determine if your client has an addiction issue, and discover what help is available for him.

CAREERS

People with executive function (EF) difficulties have been found to run into various challenges in the workplace. They may have been fired for not fulfilling job expectations, and have difficulty understanding the "unwritten rules" of the workplace. They may have personality conflicts with people at work, and they may have difficulties holding on to jobs. When discussing a client's work history, you may discover that he has worked a large variety of jobs for short periods of time, and worked multiple jobs at the same time. This is, in part, due to the fact that individuals with EF deficits are more likely than their peers to be fired from or quit their job impulsively.

SETTING LIMITS AND MANAGING TIME

When your client has executive dysfunction, it can seem like a lot of things are vying for his time. People with EF difficulties find they have "too much on their plate" on a reoccurring basis. They also have a difficult time realizing that this overload is adding to their already existing difficulties with focus. As a clinician, your job is to help your client narrow down their "busyness" and establish priorities. In Chapter 1, you learned about the executive function of organization and how difficulty establishing goals and priorities is a result of this impairment. In this section, you'll learn how to help your client set limits on their time – resulting in your client having more energy, higher productivity, and better health.

Record Your Client's Work History

Name _____   Date_____

Job Title	Company	Time Worked There	Reason for Leaving

Aspects of the client's jobs they really liked:

Aspects of the client's jobs they didn't like:

Find a Job Best Suited to Your Client's Needs

When a client has EF difficulties, they may benefit from a career with the following features:

- Fast-paced, with varied tasks each day.
- Ability to move around or travel during the work day.
- Intellectually stimulating and challenging.
- Firm due dates for projects.
- Frequent feedback and clear expectations.
- Flexible schedule.
- Immediate reinforcement for a job well done.

Jobs such as:

- firefighters
- restaurant wait staff
- teachers
- paramedics
- emergency room
- physicians
- trial attorneys
- military careers encompass many of the characteristics of ADHD-friendly jobs.

Jobs that require the following are more of a challenge:

- repetitive tasks
- lack structure
- give little feedback
- have vague expectations
- lack employer support
- have a lot of unwritten rules

For information on career inventory assessments, see the Resources section at the end of this workbook.

Discovering Your Identity

If you have executive function difficulties, you may have spent a lot of your life trying to live up to others' expectations. You may have also experienced people telling you that you weren't smart or capable, or that you were lazy. You are none of those things – you are a bright, able person. Let's get to rediscovering all the things of which you are capable!

How do you know when you are good at something?

- It feels like time flies by

- People notice your good work

- You feel a sense of accomplishment when doing that activity or task

- Even if you're getting paid to do the task, you'd do it for free

- You are "in the zone" during the task

List here the things you've done in the past that met the criteria above:

_____

_____

_____

_____

_____

_____

_____

_____

_____

Prioritizing Your Time

The Pareto Principle states that you get 80% of your results from 20% of your efforts (Dunford, Quanrong, and Tamang, 2014).

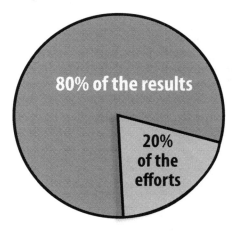

Help your client focus on the 20% that leads to the greatest results.

Which activities don't give him much of a return financially or emotionally?

_____

_____

_____

In which activities does he do well, and in which does he tend to reap the most financial and emotional benefits?

_____

_____

_____

Have your client write down tasks that he can envision doing more – tasks that he would want to do even if it was just for fun. Use the previous exercise to help guide your client. The visualization exercise on page 156 can be helpful in determining this 20% of productivity. Once your client starts contemplating what activities he wants to focus on and what he wants to cut out, follow up with the client worksheet on page 158.

What did your client learn from this exercise?

_____

_____

_____

Priority Visualization

This exercise can help your client determine which areas they should focus on at work and at home. Use the following script with your client:

"Close your eyes and take some deep breaths. Inhale and exhale. You are becoming more relaxed and focused.

I want you to visualize yourself waking up in the morning and getting ready for your day. Everything is the way you would like it to be."

Where are you?

_____

_____

_____

What city are you in?

_____

_____

_____

Do you work from home or do you go to another place to work?

_____

_____

_____

What are you working on that makes you feel productive and happy?

_____

_____

_____

How do you feel when you are doing something you enjoy?

_____

_____

_____

Now think about your ideal home life. What does it look like?

_____

_____

_____

What are you main responsibilities?

_____

_____

_____

How would you spend a relaxing evening at home?

_____

_____

_____

Close by asking:

How did this activity feel for you?

_____

_____

_____

What insights did you gain?

_____

_____

_____

Setting Limits on Your Time

When you have executive function difficulties, it is difficult to manage your time. You also may want to get involved in a variety of activities but wind up overloading yourself.

When someone asks you to get involved with something, ask yourself the following questions:

- Is this in my best interest?

- Does this help me work towards a goal?

- Will this take up a large part of my time?

- What rewards will I get from this activity?

- Does this interfere with any already scheduled activity?

Saying "no" may upset friends and family when you first start setting limits. This is because you are changing up the *dynamics* or rules of the relationship of the relationship. However, over time you'll find that people tend to respect you and your time more. If you have some friends or family who still don't respect your time, consider limiting your interactions with them.

DELEGATION

While you are with your client, help him come up with tasks at home that are important but that he doesn't necessarily have to do – tasks that can be delegated to someone else. This can include cleaning the house and mowing the lawn. There are a couple of challenges individuals with EF difficulties face when considering delegating. First, if they've never tried it before it can be somewhat daunting; second, they may not be sure if someone else can do as good of a job as they do. It is important to point out that no one gets through life alone – asking for help is a strength, not a weakness. Just like a CEO has support staff, your client needs support as well.

A good way to help your client think of tasks to delegate is to have him write down any weekly tasks that he was doing which resulted in thoughts such as, "I really dislike doing this," "I'm not very good at this," "This is something I'm really wasting my time with," or "I could be using my time better elsewhere." Delegating means hiring or bartering with someone so you have more time to do the things you want to do and are good at, and so you can spend less time doing the things you aren't so good at. Other examples of tasks that can be delegated besides mowing the lawn and cleaning the house include:

- Walking the dog
- Home repairs
- Pressure washing
- Grocery shopping
- Setting up money management software
- Making sure bills are paid
- Organizing files and clutter

Your client may wonder where to get someone to help with these tasks. Your client may also say that he doesn't have enough money to hire someone. Besides paying someone to help, other options include enlisting the help of a trusted friend or family member or bartering with someone. Hiring a person to help can improve your client's quality of life.

Hiring a Helper

You've talked with your clinician about delegating or "farming out" tasks in order to reduce your stress and have a good quality of life. So how do you find a person to help you out? You have a few options:

- Ask a trusted friend or family member to help.

- Barter – someone helps you in exchange for you helping them.

- Hire someone.

If you do ask a friend or family member, that "trusted" part is important. You want someone who keeps your household information confidential and doesn't talk about it with other members of your family or other friends.

Let's say you've decided to hire someone. Ask your friends and family who they recommend. College students can be great helpers – they need the money, and you need the help. They also may be driven due to the fact that they need job experience on their resumé.

You can also place an ad on an app or website like NextDoor or Craigslist. Craigslist has the added benefit of being anonymous. In your ad, mention the following:

- Give a brief description of tasks – light cleaning, help with organizing, walking the dogs.

- Note if you have pets, including what kind - "two large dogs," for example.

- State that the helper needs reliable transportation.

- State how many hours you need them to work – some people start out hiring someone for four hours a week and then increase the hours as needed.

- State what days you need them and what times. Even something like "Monday mornings and Wednesday evenings" is acceptable.

- State the hourly rate you will pay. Look at similar ads in your community to find out the "going rate."

- State that the person needs to be a self-starter. This means that they aren't constantly coming to you to ask you what they should do next – the person you need gets into a routine and knows what to do without you asking.

- Have people email you their resumé. Again, if you are using Craigslist, you get an anonymous email that forwards to your email.

Note that you don't have to say anything about having ADHD, Asperger's, anxiety, or another issue – that is your private medical information. If you are using Craigslist, putting your ad under the Gigs sections for free. Once you get responses, delete any resumés that have spelling or grammar errors. You need someone who is detail-oriented, because that's an area in which you need help.

In addition, delete any emails that do not contain a resumé either as an attachment or in the body of the email. You need someone who follows directions. Now narrow down your choices to two or three people. Email them and say you would like to meet at a coffee shop or other public place for a quick interview. Trust your intuition – if you meet with someone and something seems "off," do not hire this person. If you like one of the people with whom you meet, do a background check. If everything checks out, welcome your new assistant!

CREATING A STRUCTURED ROUTINE

If your client has difficulties with time management, sticking to a routine can be very helpful. When your client knows what to expect each day, it really improves his quality of life. Work with your client to set up a weekly schedule. Using Gmail calendar or another type of interactive calendar, work with your client to block off times for the following:

- Breakfast, lunch, and dinner
- Exercise
- Commuting
- Work
- Classes
- Studying
- Chores (like laundry and grocery shopping)
- Extracurricular activities (like social groups, sports, and business networking)
- Free time

Use a different color for each task. For example, all studying times are in yellow, all exercise times are in green, and so on. Color-coding is a great help to people with executive dysfunction, and especially for people who have a comorbid reading disability. Here are some tips for creating your client's schedule:

- First ask them what set (fixed) activities they have each week. This helps establish a framework for your calendar.
- If your client is a college student, schedule time for studying directly after class – this is an excellent time to review class notes and make any edits.
- Remember to schedule in meal times. People with EF difficulties have a tendency to skip meals due to hyperfocus and/or distraction.
- Check in with your client regularly about their schedule, and update accordingly.

When you use a shared online calendar such as on Gmail, there is built-in privacy for both you and your client. Your client can't see your other Gmail calendars, and you can't see your client's other calendars.

FINANCIAL ISSUES

If a client has executive dysfunction, they may have issues with impulsive spending, difficulty organizing financial documents, and not keeping track of spending. Clients also may not have established an emergency fund, nor have they taken advantage of their employer's retirement plan, like a 401(k) (Sarkis and Klein, 2009).

If you are working with a person with EF difficulties, you may encounter the following:

- Disorganization of financial papers.
- Not keeping track of purchases from a joint account.

- Not keeping money management software or apps up-to-date.
- Debt from impulsive spending.
- Compulsive spending or compulsive saving (as a compensation strategy).
- Buying high-priced items without thinking it over first.
- Investing in "get rich quick" schemes.
- Having problems with gambling.
- Lack of money saved up for their children's education.

Co-therapy with a Financial Professional

One type of therapeutic modality is to have a financial professional in the room with you while you are doing therapy. The financial professional could be a certified public accountant (CPA) or certified financial planner (CFP), amongst other financial professionals. During this type of cotherapy session, you do the counseling piece, and the financial professional gives their advice about the financial situation. People with impulsivity and poor financial decision-making tend to like this type of therapy because it is "one-stop shopping" and done in the comfort of the therapist's office. In order to find financial professionals in your community, ask for referrals from other clinicians and also see the Resources section at the end of this workbook.

Budgeting

Budgeting can be very difficult for people with executive dysfunction. Budgeting involves the following executive functions: planning, organization, forethought, and learning from consequences. Budgeting also requires arithmetic skills, and a large number of people with executive dysfunction also have a math learning disability. Some money management books have detailed budget worksheets that are difficult for people with even good EFs to follow. The following worksheet is a budget for your clients that is broken down into easy categories.

Creating a Budget

Use the following activity to determine your monthly budget. You don't need to get the amounts down to the penny. Just writing a dollar amount is fine.

Using your notebook, begin by writing down your monthly income. Because many people with executive dysfunction have difficulties with math, here are some formulas for figuring out your monthly income:

- Weekly pay times four

- Bimonthly pay times two

- If your income varies widely from month to month, find out the yearly total and divide by 12.

Now make a list like the one below and fill in your fixed and flexible expenses in your notebook. Fixed expenses are those for which you pay a set amount from month to month. Flexible expenses are those that you have some leeway in the amount you are paying. If you pay your car insurance every six months, divide that payment by six to get your monthly payment. Remember that this budget is just a guideline. Feel free to add or delete items as you see fit.

INCOME

Job 1 _____

Job 2 _____

Other income _____

Total: _____

FIXED EXPENSES

Car payment _____

Rent _____

Cable _____

Internet _____

Electricity _____

Gas _____

Telephone _____

Tuition _____

Car insurance _____

Health insurance _____

Medications _____

Fuel (gasoline) _____

Child support _____

Alimony _____

Total: _____

FLEXIBLE EXPENSES

Eating out _____

Snacks _____

Vacations/trips _____

Concerts/music _____

Game tickets _____

Groceries _____

Clothing _____

Gifts _____

Hobbies _____

TOTAL: _____

Total of fixed plus flexible expenses: _____

Income minus expenses: _____

Your main goal is to have money left over after you subtract your expenses from your income.

DEALING WITH ADDICTION

People with executive dysfunction are more likely to abuse alcohol and other drugs, including caffeine, nicotine, alcohol, marijuana, cocaine, and even prescription drugs. In fact, one in five adults with ADHD has experienced substance abuse (Wilens et al., 2007). There is also a much higher rate of executive dysfunction, particularly ADHD, among addicts than in the general population (Wilens et al., 2006). Individuals with EF issues also start using drugs at an earlier age and have more intense use than those without EF issues (Wilens et al., 2005). It is also more difficult for people with EF difficulties to quit using substances and then stay abstinent.

As you read in Chapter 1, executive dysfunction can be, in part, caused by a low level of neurotransmitters. A client will try to find a way to raise those low levels, whether consciously or unconsciously. Additionally, the stress of having EF difficulties can cause individuals to turn to substances as a means by which to self-soothe and relieve their difficulties. For those with EF difficulties, using substances may lead them to feeling as if their brain is functioning "normally" for a brief period of time. However, those effects do not last, and dependence can lead to withdrawal symptoms when they try to stop. As you learned in Chapter 3, prescribed medication is a safer, regulated, and less addictive way to help the brain replace the chemicals it needs.

Caffeine

Caffeine is one of the most widely abused drugs among individuals with executive dysfunction. First, it can help with focus, although the effect only lasts for about 30 minutes. Secondly, it is a drug habit that is socially encouraged – look at how many social practices revolve around coffee. However, the side effects of caffeine withdrawal do not outweigh the benefits. Caffeine withdrawal symptoms include stomachaches, irritable bowel problems, headaches, vomiting, nervousness, and insomnia. If a client wants to wean off of caffeine, it is recommended that you have them speak with their doctor. Gradually reducing caffeine will help ease some of the withdrawal symptoms.

Signs of Addiction

If you think you may have a problem with addiction, it may be helpful to learn exactly what it means to be "addicted." When you are addicted to something, you may build up a *tolerance* to the drug and you may also experience *withdrawal* symptoms.

TOLERANCE

- When you need more and more of a substance in order to get the same effect from it, you are building up a tolerance.

- A single marijuana joint isn't getting you high anymore; now you need two or even three to get the same effect.

- The amount of time it takes your mind and body to build up tolerance depends on the substance that is being abused, the amount you use each time, and how frequently you use it.

WITHDRAWAL

- Withdrawal comes in two forms – psychological and physiological.

- Withdrawal happens when you have a psychological (mind) or physiological (body) reaction when you cut back or stop using a substance.

- You can experience psychological withdrawal symptoms, such as aggression, confusion, and paranoia. You can also experience the physiological effects of withdrawal, including nausea, shaking, and seizures.

IS YOUR CLIENT HAVING ADDICTION ISSUES?

When reviewing your client's history, answer the following questions:

- Have they needed more and more of the substance in order to achieve the intended effect?
- Do they hide their substance abuse from friends and family?
- Do they regularly associate with other people who abuse substances?
- Do they ever "black out" and not remember events that happened during use?
- Have they ever lied or stolen in order to obtain the substance?
- Have friends and/or family expressed concern over their substance use?
- Has the substance use affected work or school performance?
- Have attempts to quit not been successful?

If your client was positive for any of these questions, addiction is a possibility for your client.

Addiction Treatment

It is recommended that addiction issues are treated and resolved before continuing treatment specifically for EF issues. Addiction issues can "mask" executive dysfunction, so it can be difficult to tell what is the addiction and what is an EF issue. Once the addiction is treated, the clinician is able to see the "true" level of executive dysfunction. Treatment includes referral to a clinician who specializes in addiction or to an addiction treatment center.

Appendix A
Executive Function Assessment Tools

Name	Type	Rated by
Stroop Color-Word Test	EF Performance: Interference	Clinician or Computer
WCST	EF Performance: Set Shifting	Clinician or Computer
Tower of London	EF Performance	Clinician or computer
IVA	EF Performance	Computer
TOVA	EF Performance	Computer
Quotient Test	EF Performance	Clinician
BRIEF-A	EF Rating Scale	Clinician
FrSBe	EF Rating Scale	Clinician
BDEFS for Adults	EF Rating Scale	Clinician
CPT 3	EF Performance	Clinician

Appendix B
Moulton Screener of Executive Function Impairment

Ask your client to answer the following questions with a "yes" or "no." These questions apply if this is a current issue or an issue that has happened in the past.

WORKING MEMORY

    1. Do you have difficulty doing tasks that require you to remember rules and then act on them?

    2. Do you have difficulty with tasks that require you to follow multiple steps?

TIME MANAGEMENT

    1. Do you show up late to work or events even though you try your hardest to show up on time?

    2. Do you over or underestimate how much time it takes to complete tasks?

EMOTION REGULATION

    1. Do your family or friends say that you get frustrated or angry easily?

    2. Do your family or friends say that you get too excited or "wound up" about things, and you start speaking too loudly?

COGNITIVE FLEXIBILITY

    1. Do you have difficulty adjusting when someone changes the rules of a game you are playing?

    2. Do you have difficulty coming up with alternative plans while driving if there is an accident or road block on your regular route?

PLANNING

1. Do you return back to your home after you've left for work because you've forgotten something?
2. Do you have money saved up for your future?

FORETHOUGHT

1. Do you have difficulty playing strategy-related games like chess and checkers?
2. Do you have difficulty weighing options?

LEARNING FROM CONSEQUENCES

1. Do you seem to be making the same mistakes over and over?
2. Have you been in legal trouble? (Arrests, speeding tickets, warrants)

ORGANIZATION

1. Is your home and/or office cluttered?
2. Do you have difficulties making outlines?

RECONSTITUTION OF INFORMATION

1. Has your spouse told you to get certain items from the store and you came back with different items?
2. Do you have issues with friendships because your friends will tell you when to meet up and you have the wrong day or time?

The more questions your client answers "yes" to, the more likely there is an executive function impairment in that area.

Appendix C
Recommended Books

Barkley, R. A. (Ed.) (2014). *Attention-Deficit Hyperactivity Disorder: A Handbook for Diagnosis and Treatment.* New York: Guilford Press.

Barkley, R. A., Murphy, K. R., & Fischer, M. (2010). *ADHD in Adults: What the Science Says.* New York: Guilford Press.

Bourne, E. J. (2011). *The Anxiety and Phobia Workbook.* Oakland, CA: New Harbinger Publications, Inc.

Hallowell, E. & Ratey, J. (2011). *Driven to Distraction: Recognizing and Coping with Attention Deficit Hyperactivity Disorder (Rev.).* New York: Anchor.

Hanh, T. N. (1991). *Peace is Every Step.* New York: Bantam Books.

Honos-Webb, L. (2008). *The Gift of Adult ADD: How to Transform Your Challenges & Build on Your Strengths.* Oakland, CA: New Harbinger Publications, Inc.

Kelly, K. & Ramundo, P. (2006). *You Mean I'm Not Lazy, Stupid or Crazy?!: The Classic Self-help Book for Adults with Attention Deficit Disorder.* New York: Scribner.

Kolberg, J. (1998). *Conquering Chronic Disorganization.* Decatur, GA: Squall Press, Inc.

Kolberg, J. & Nadeau, K. (2002). *ADD-friendly Ways to Organize Your Life.* New York: Routledge.

Orlov, M. (2010). *The ADHD Effect on Marriage: Understand and Rebuild Your Relationship in Six Steps.* Plantation, FL: Specialty Press, Inc.

Novotni, M. (2001). *What Does Everyone Know That I Don't?: Social Skills Help for Adults with Attention Deficit/Hyperactivity Disorder (AD/HD).* Plantation, FL: Specialty Press, Inc.

Ramsey, J. R. (2010). *Nonmedication Treatments for Adult ADHD: Evaluating Impact On Daily Functioning and Well-Being.* Washington, DC: American Psychological Association.

Sarkis, S. (2015). *Natural Relief for Adult ADHD: Complementary Strategies for Increasing Focus, Attention, and Motivation With or Without Medication.* Oakland, CA: New Harbinger Publications, Inc.

Sarkis, S. (2008). *Making the Grade with ADD: A Student's Guide to Succeeding in College with Attention Deficit Disorder.* Oakland, CA: New Harbinger Publications, Inc.

Sarkis, S. (2011). *10 Simple Solutions to Adult ADD: How to Overcome Chronic Distraction & Accomplish Your Goals,* 2nd edition. Oakland, CA: New Harbinger Publications, Inc.

Sarkis, S. (2011). *Adult ADD: A Guide for the Newly Diagnosed.* Oakland, CA: New Harbinger Publications, Inc.

Sarkis, S. & Klein, K. (2009). *ADD and Your Money: A Guide to Personal Finance for Adults with Attention-Deficit Disorder.* Oakland, CA: New Harbinger Publications, Inc.

Tuckman, A. (2012). *Understand Your Brain, Get More Done: The ADHD Executive Functions Workbook.* Plantation, FL: Specialty Press, Inc.

Tuckman, A. (2009). *More Attention, Less Deficit: Success Strategies for Adults with ADHD.* Plantation, FL: Specialty Press, Inc.

Zylowska, L. (2012). *The Mindfulness Prescription for Adult ADHD: An 8-Step Program for Strengthening Attention, Managing Emotions, and Achieving Your Goals.* Boston: Trumpeter.

Resources

ADHD

Attention Deficit Disorder Association   www.add.org

Children and Adults with Attention Deficit Hyperactivity Disorder (CHADD)
www.chadd.org

CHADD National Resource Center on ADHD   www.help4adhd.org

Anxiety and Depression

Anxiety and Depression Association of America   www.adaa.org

Depression and Bipolar Support Alliance   www.dbsalliance.org

Careers

Holland Code Quiz   www.roguecc.edu/Counseling/HollandCodes/test.asp

Occupational Outlook Handbook   www.bls.gov/ooh/

U.S. Department of Labor Blog   https://blog.dol.gov/tag/ooh/

Accommodations

College

Association on Higher Education and Disability (AHEAD)   www.ahead.org

National Center for College Students with Disabilities   www.nccsdonline.org

Smartpens

Livescribe   www.livescribe.com

Workplace

Americans with Disabilities Act (ADA)   www.ada.gov

U.S. Department of Justice

1-800-514-0301 (ADA Information Line)

The ADA: Your Employment Rights   www.eeoc.gov/facts/ada18.html

Exercise

Fitocracy app   www.fitocracy.com

Runkeeper app   www.runkeeper.com

Ramblr app   www.ramblr.com

Mindfulness Meditation

Buddhify app   www.buddhify.com

Headspace app   www.headspace.com

Money

Quicken Software   www.quicken.com

Mint app   www.mint.com

Organizing

National Association of Professional Organizers   http://www.napo.net

Social Skills

Succeed Socially   www.succeedsocially.com

Supplements

Consumer Lab   www.consumerlab.com

Omega 3-6-9

University of Maryland Medical Center

http://umm.edu/health/medical/altmed/supplement/omega3-fatty-acids

http://umm.edu/health/medical/altmed/supplement/omega6-fatty-acids

http://umm.edu/health/medical/altmed/supplement/omega9-fatty-acids

References

For your convenience, purchasers can download and print
worksheets and handouts from www.pesi.com/EF Adults

Adler, L., Tanaka, Y., Williams, D., Trzepacz, P. T., Goto, T., Allen, A. J., Escobar, R., & Upadhyaya, H. P. (2014). Executive function in adults with attention-deficit/hyperactivity disorder during treatment with atomoxetine in a randomized, placebo-controlled, withdrawal study. *Journal of Clinical Psychopharmacology*, 34(4): 461–466.

Ali, A., Weiss, T., Dutton, A., Hua, A., Jones, K., Kashikar-Zuck, S., … Shapiro, E. (2016). Mindfulness-Based Stress Reduction (MBSR) for adolescents with chronic pain: A pilot study. *The Journal of Pain*, 17(4), S101.

Altarac, M., & Saroha, E. (2007). Lifetime prevalence of learning disability among U.S. children. *Pediatrics*, 119(Supplement 1), S77-S83.

Alzheimer's Association (2016). 2016 Alzheimer's Disease facts and figures. *Alzheimer's & Dementia*, 2016;12(4).

American Psychiatric Association. (2013). *Diagnostic and Statistical Manual of Mental Disorders* (5th ed.). Washington, DC: Author.

Anatalis, C. J., Stevens, L. J., Campbell, M., Pazdro, R., Ericson, K., & Burgess, J. R. (2006). Omega-3 fatty acid status in attention-deficit/hyperactivity disorder. *Prostaglandins, Leukotrienes and Essential Fatty Acids*, 75(4–5):299–308.

Antshel, K. M., & Barkley, R. A. (2008). Psychosocial interventions in attention deficit hyperactivity disorder. *Child and Adolescent Psychiatric Clinics of North America*, 17(2): 421-437.

Antshel, K. M., Faraone, S. V., Maglione, K., Doyle, A. E., Fried, R., Seidman, L. J., & Biederman, J. (2010). Executive functioning in high-IQ adults with ADHD. *Psychological Medicine*, 40(11): 1909-1918.

Antshel, K. M., Hargrave, T. M., Simonescu, M., Kaul, P., Hendricks, K., & Faraone, S. V. (2011). Advances in understanding and treating ADHD. *BMC Medicine*, 9(1):72.

Archer, T., & Kostrzewa, R. M. (2012). Physical exercise alleviates ADHD symptoms: Regional deficits and development trajectory. *Neurotoxicity Research*, 21(2): 195-209.

Ardila, A., Rosselli, M., Matute, E., & Guajardo, S. (2005). The influence of the parents' educational level on the development of executive functions. *Developmental Neuropsychology*, 28(1): 539-560.

Bader, A., & Adesman, A. (2012). Complementary and alternative therapies for children and adolescents with ADHD. *Current Opinion In Pediatrics*,24(6): 760-769.

Barkley, R. A., Fischer, M., Smallish, L., & Fletcher, K. (2005). Young adult outcome of hyperactive children: Adaptive functioning in major life activities. *Journal of the American Academy of Child and Adolescent Psychiatry*, 45(2): 192–202.

Barkley, R. A. (2005). *Attention-Deficit Hyperactivity Disorder: A Handbook for Diagnosis and Treatment*, 3rd ed. New York: The Guilford Press.

Barragán, E., Breuer, D., & Döpfner, M. (2014). Efficacy and safety of omega-3/6 fatty acids, methylphenidate, and a combined treatment in children with ADHD. *Journal of Attention Disorders*, Epub ahead of print.

Bauer, I., Crewther, S., Pipingas, A., Sellick, L., & Crewther, D. (2014). Does omega-3 fatty acid supplementation enhance neural efficiency? A review of the literature. *Human Psychopharmacology*, 29(1): 8–18.

Bauer, B. A., Tilburt, J. C., Sood, A., Li, G., & Wang, S. (2016). Complementary and alternative medicine therapies for chronic pain. *Chinese Journal of Integrative Medicine*, 22(6): 403–411. http://doi.org/10.1007/ s11655-016-2258-y

Beck, J. S. (2011). *Cognitive-Behavior Therapy: Basics and Beyond* (2nd ed.). New York: The Guilford Press.

Beebe, D. W. (2005). Neurobehavioral effects of obstructive sleep apnea: An overview and heuristic model. *Current Opinion in Pulmonary Medicine*, 11(6): 494-500.

Biederman, J. (2003). Pharmacotherapy for attention-deficit/hyperactivity disorder (ADHD) decreases the risk for substance abuse: Findings from a longitudinal follow-up of youths with and without ADHD. *Journal of Clinical Psychiatry*, 64(Suppl. 11): 3-8.

Biederman, J., Melmed, R. D., Patel, A., McBurnett, K., Konow, J., Lyne, A., & Scherer, N. (2008). A randomized, double-blind, placebo-controlled study of guanfacine extended release in children and adolescents with attention-deficit/hyperactivity disorder. *Pediatrics*, 121(1): e73-e84.

Biederman, J., Monuteaux, M. C., Spencer, T., Wilens, T. E., Macpherson, H. A., & Faraone, S. V. (2008). Stimulant therapy and risk for subsequent substance use disorders in male adults with ADHD: A naturalistic controlled 10-year follow-up study. *American Journal of Psychiatry*, 165(5): 597-603.

Biljenga, D., Van Someren, E. J., Gruber, R., Bron, T. I., Kruithof, I. F., Spanbroek, E. C., & Kooij, J. J. (2013). Body temperature, activity and melatonin profiles in adults with attention-deficit/hyperactivity disorder and delayed sleep: A case–control study. *Journal of Sleep Research*, 22(6): 607-616.

Blesch, L., & Breese McCoy, S. J. (2013). Obstructive sleep apnea mimics attention deficit disorder. *Journal of Attention Disorders*, Epub ahead of print.

Brown, T. E. (2009). ADHD/ADHD and impaired executive function in clinical practice. *Current Attention Disorders Reports*, 1(1): 37–41.

Brown, T. E., Holdnack, J., Saylor, K., Adler, L., Spencer, T., Williams, D. W., Padival, A. K., Schuh, K., & Trezepacz, P. T. (2011). Effects of atomoxetine on executive function impairments in adults with ADHD. *Journal of Attention Disorders*, 15(2): 130-138.

Bush, G., Spencer, T. J., Holmes, J., Shin, L. M., Valera, E. M., Seidman, L. J., Makris, N., Surman, C., Aleardi, M., Mick, E., & Biederman, J. (2008). Functional magnetic resonance imaging of methylphenidate and placebo in attention-deficit/hyperactivity disorder during the multi-source interference task. *Archives of General Psychiatry*, 65(1): 102-114.

Caldwell, K., Emery, L., Harrison, M., & Greeson, J. (2011). Changes in mindfulness, well-being, and sleep quality in college students through taijiquan courses: A cohort control study. *Journal of Alternative and Complementary Medicine*, 17: 931-938.

Carvalho, C., Caetano, J. M., Cunha, L., Rebouta, P., Kaptchuk, T. J., & Kirsch, I. (2016). Open-label placebo treatment in chronic low back pain: A randomized controlled trial. *Pain*, 157(12), 2766.

Castonguay, N., Lussier, M., Bugaiska, A., Lord, C., & Bherer, L. (2015). Executive functions in men and postmenopausal women. *Journal of Clinical and Experimental Neuropsychology*: 37(2), 193-208.

Center for Behavioral Health Statistics and Quality. (2016). *Key substance use and mental health indicators in the United States: Results from the 2015 National Survey on Drug Use and Health* (HHS Publication No. SMA 16-4984, NSDUH Series H-51). Retrieved from http://www.samhsa.gov/data/

Calvo, A., & Bialystok, E. (2014). Independent effects of bilingualism and socioeconomic status on language ability and executive functioning. *Cognition*, 130(3): 278-288.

Centers for Disease Control and Prevention. (2016, April 1). Prevalence and characteristics of autism spectrum disorder among children aged 8 years — Autism and Developmental Disabilities Monitoring Network, 11 Sites, United States, 2012. *Surveillance Summaries*, 65(3); 1–23.

Centers for Disease Control and Prevention. (2011). Effect of short sleep duration on daily activities – United States, 2005-2008. *Morbidity and Mortality Weekly Report*, 60(8): 239–42. http://www.ncbi.nlm.nih.gov/pubmed/21368739.

Chiesa, A., & Malinowski, P. (2011). Mindfulness-based approaches: Are they all the same? *Journal of Clinical Psychology*, 67(4): 404–424.

Chang, Z., Lichtenstein, P., Halldner, L., D'Onofrio, B., Serlachius, E., Fazel, S., Langstrom, N., & Larsson,

H. (2014). Stimulant ADHD medication and risk for substance abuse. *Journal of Child Psychology and Psychiatry*, 55(8): 878-885.

Coghill, D. (2010). The impact of medication on quality of life in adults with attention-deficit hyperactivity disorder: A systematic review. *CNS Drugs*, 24(10): 843-866.

Colby, S. L., & Ortman, J. M. (2015). Projections of the Size and Composition of the U.S. Population: 2014 to 2060. *U.S. Census Bureau*, 25-1143.

Converse, A. K., Ahlers, E. O., Travers, B. G., & Davidson, R. J. (2014). Tai chi training reduces self-report of inattention in healthy young adults. *Frontiers in Human Neuroscience*, 8:13.

Cooper, W. O., Habel, L. A., Sox, C. M., Chan, K. A., Arbogast, P. G., & Cheetham, T. C. (2011). ADHD drugs and serious cardiovascular events in children and young adults. *New England Journal of Medicine*, 365: 1896-1904.

Cortese, S., & Vincenzi, B. (2012). Obesity and ADHD: Clinical and neurobiological implications. In *Behavioral Neuroscience of Attention Deficit Hyperactivity Disorder and Its Treatment*. Edited by Stanford, C., & Tannock, R. New York: Springer.

Cruz, M. P. (2010). Guanfacine extended-release tablets (Intuniv): A nonstimulant selective alpha$_{2A}$-adrenergic receptor agonist for attention-deficit/hyperactivity disorder. *Pharmacy and Therapeutics*, 35(8): 448-451.

Curtis, P., & Gaylord, S. (2005). Safety issues in the interaction of conventional, complementary, and alternative health care. *Complementary Health Practice Review*, 10(1): 3–31.

Daubenmier, J., Kristeller, J., Hecht, F. M., Maninger, N., Kuwata, M., Jhaveri, K., ... & Epel, E. (2011). Mindfulness intervention for stress eating to reduce cortisol and abdominal fat among overweight and obese women: An exploratory randomized controlled study. *Journal of Obesity*, 2011.

Davis, C. (2010). Attention-deficit/hyperactivity disorder: Associations with overeating and obesity. *Current Psychiatry Reports*, 12(5): 389–95.

Durston, S. (2010). Imaging genetics in ADHD. *Neuroimage*, 53: 832-838.

Eakin, L., Minde, K., Hechtman, L., Ochs, E., Krane, E., Bouffard, R., Greenfield, B., & Looper, K. (2004). The marital and family functioning of adults with ADHD and their spouses. *Journal of Attention Disorders*, 8(1):1-10.

Elia, J., Gai, X., Xie, H. M., Perin, J. C., Geiger, E., Glessner, J. T., ... & Muganga, B. M. (2010). Rare structural variants found in attention-deficit hyperactivity disorder are preferentially associated with neurodevelopmental genes. *Molecular Psychiatry*, 15(6): 637-646.

Esch, T., Duckstein, J., Welke, J., & Braun, V. (2007). Mind/body techniques for physiological and psychological stress management via tai chi training – a pilot study. *Medical Science Monitor*, 13: BR488-BR497.

Fagundo, A. B., De La Torre, R., Jiménez-Murcia, S., Agüera, Z., Granero, R., Tárrega, S., ... & Forcano, L. (2012). Executive functions profile in extreme eating/weight conditions: From anorexia nervosa to obesity. *PloS one*, 7(8): e43382.

Faraone, S. V., & Glatt, S. J. (2010). A comparison of the efficacy of medications for adult attention-deficit/hyperactivity disorder using meta-analysis of effect sizes. *The Journal of Clinical Psychiatry*, 71(6): 754-763.

Faul, M., Xu, L., Wald, M. M., & Coronado, V. G. (2010). Traumatic brain injury in the United States: Emergency department visits, hospitalizations and deaths 2002-2006. *Atlanta, GA: Centers for Disease Control and Prevention, National Center for Injury Prevention and Control*.

Fisher, B. C. (2013). The overlap of sleep apnea and ADHD/ADHD. In *Attention Deficit Disorder: Practical Coping Mechanisms*. Edited by Fisher, B. C. Boca Raton, FL: CRC Press.

Fossum, I. N., Nordnes, L. T., Storemark, S. S., Bjorvatn, B., & Pallesen, S. (2014). The association between use of electronic media in bed before going to sleep and insomnia symptoms, daytime sleepiness, morningness, and chronotype. *Behavioral Sleep Medicine*, 12(5): 343-357.

Foti, F. S., Wahlstrom, J. L., & Wienkers, L. C. (2007). The in vitro drug interaction potential of dietary supplements containing multiple herbal components. *Drug Metabolism & Disposition*, 35(2): 185–188.

Fuglestad, A. J., Whitley, M. L., Carlson, S. M., Boys, C. J., Eckerle, J. K., Fink, B. A., & Wozniak, J. R. (2015). Executive functioning deficits in preschool children with Fetal Alcohol Spectrum Disorders. *Child Neuropsychology*, 21(6): 716-731.

Garcia, J. R., MacKillop, J., Aller, E. L., Merriwether, A. M., Wilson, D. S., & Lum, J. K. (2010). Associations between dopamine D4 receptor gene variation with both infidelity and sexual promiscuity. *PLoS ONE*, 5(11): e14162.

Garcia-Cazarin, M. L., Wambogo, E. A., Regan, K. S., & Davis, C. D. (2014). Dietary supplement research portfolio at the NIH, 2009-2011. *The Journal of Nutrition*, 144(4): 414–8. doi:10.3945/jn.113.189803

Gavett, B. E., Stern, R. A., & McKee, A. C. (2011). Chronic Traumatic Encephalopathy: A Potential Late Effect of Sport-Related Concussive and Subconcussive Head Trauma. *Clinics in Sports Medicine*, 30(1): 179–xi. http://doi.org/10.1016/j.csm.2010.09.007

Gawrilow, C., Stadler, G., Langguth, N., Naumann, A., & Boeck, A. (2016). Physical activity, affect, and cognition in children with symptoms of ADHD. *Journal of Attention Disorders*, 20(2): 151-162.

Gjervan, B., Torgersen, T., Nordahl, H. M., & Rasmussen, K. (2012). Functional impairment and occupational outcome in adults with ADHD. *Journal of Attention Disorders*, 16(7): 544-52.

Goel, N., Rao, H., Durmer, J. S., & Dinges, D. F. (2009). Neurocognitive consequences of sleep deprivation. *Seminars in Neurology* 29(4): 320-339.

Goncalves, P. D., Ometto, M., Bechara, A., Malbergier, A., Amaral, R., Nicastri, S., ... & Andrade, A. G. (2014). Motivational Interviewing combined with chess accelerates improvement in executive functions in cocaine dependent patients: A one-month prospective study. *Drug and Alcohol Dependence*, 141: 79-84.

Graham, D. I., & Gennareli, T. A. (2000). Chapter 5, "Pathology of Brain Damage After Head Injury." In, Cooper, P., & Golfinos, G. *Head Injury*, 4th Ed. Morgan Hill: New York.

Gow, R. V., & Hibbeln, J. R. (2014). Omega-3 & treatment implications in Attention Deficit Hyperactivity Disorder (ADHD) and associated behavioral symptoms. *Lipid Technology*, 26(1): 7–10.

Grassman, V., Alves, M. V., Santos-Galduroz, R. F., and Galduroz, J. C. F. (2014). Possible cognitive benefits of acute physical exercise in children with ADHD: A systematic review. *Journal of Attention Disorders*, Epub ahead of print.

Groeger, J. A., Viola, A. U., Lo, J. C., von Schantz, M., Archer, S. N., & Dijk, D. J. (2008). Early morning executive functioning during sleep deprivation is compromised by a PERIOD3 polymorphism. *Sleep*, 31(8): 1159-1167.

Grosswald, S. J., Stixrud, W. R., Travis, F., & Bateh, M. A. (2008). Use of the transcendental meditation technique to reduce symptoms of attention deficit hyperactivity disorder (ADHD) by reducing stress and anxiety: An exploratory study. *Current Issues in Education*, 10(2): 1-16.

Guan, L., Wang, B., Chen, Y., Yang, L., Li, J., Qian, Q., ... & Wang, Y. (2009). A high-density single-nucleotide polymorphism screen of 23 candidate genes in attention deficit hyperactivity disorder: Suggesting multiple susceptibility genes among Chinese Han population. *Molecular Psychiatry*, 14(5): 546-554.

Halmey, A., Fasmer, O. B., Gillberg, C., & Haavik, J. (2009). Occupational outcome in adult ADHD: Impact of symptom profile, comorbid psychiatric problems, and treatment. *Journal of Attention Disorders*, 13(2): 175–187.

Hammerness, P., McCarthy, K., Mancuso, E., Gendron, C., & Geller, D. (2009). Atomoxetine for the treatment of attention-deficit/hyperactivity disorder in children and adolescents: A review. *Neuropsychiatr Dis Treat*, 5: 215-226.

Hanh, T. N. (1991). *Peace is Every Step*. New York: Bantam Books.

Hariprasad, V. R., Arasappa, R., Varambally, S., Srinath, S., and Gangadhar, B. N. (2013). Feasibility and efficacy of yoga as an add-on intervention in attention deficit-hyperactivity disorder: An exploratory study. *Indian Journal of Psychiatry*, 55(Suppl 3): S379-S384.

Hawkey, E., & Nigg, J. T. (2014). Omega-3 fatty acid and ADHD: Blood level analysis and meta-analytic extension of supplementation trials. *Clinical Psychology Review*.

Heffner, J. L., Lewis, D. F., & Winhusen, T. M. (2013). Osmotic release oral system methylphenidate prevents weight gain during a smoking-cessation attempt in adults with ADHD. *Nicotine & Tobacco Research:*

Official Journal of the Society for Research on Nicotine and Tobacco, 15(2): 583–7.

Hirshkowitz, M., Whiton, K., Albert, S. M., Alessi, C., Bruni, O., DonCarlos, L., ... & Neubauer, D. N. (2015). National Sleep Foundation's sleep time duration recommendations: Methodology and results summary. *Sleep Health*, 1(1): 40-43.

Holvoet, E., & Gabriëls, L. (2012). Disturbed sleep in children with ADHD: is there a place for melatonin as a treatment option? *Tijdschrift voor Psychiatrie*, 55(5): 349-357.

Hölzel, B. K., Carmody, J., Vangel, M., Congleton, C., Yerramsetti, S. M., Gard, T., & Lazar, S. W. (2011). Mindfulness practice leads to increases in regional brain gray matter density. *Psychiatry Research*, 191(1): 36–43.

Hurt, E. A., Arnold, L. E., & Lofthouse, N. (2011). Dietary and nutritional treatments for attention-deficit/hyperactivity disorder: Current research support and recommendations for practitioners. *Current Psychiatry Reports*, 13(5): 323–332.

Huss, M., Volp, A., & Stauss-Grabo, M. (2010). Supplementation of polyunsaturated fatty acids, magnesium, and zinc....seeking medical advice for attention-deficit / hyperactivity problems – an observational cohort study. *Children Seeking Lipids Health Dis*, 9: 105.

Iglesias, S. L., Azzara, S., Granchetti, H., Lagomarsino, E., & Vigo, D. E. (2014). Anxiety, anger, salivary cortisol and cardiac autonomic activity in palliative care professionals with and without mind–body training experience: Results from a pilot study. *European Journal of Integrative Medicine*, 6(1): 98–103.

Infurna, M. R., Brunner, R., Holz, B., Parzer, P., Giannone, F., Reichl, C., ... & Kaess, M. (2016). The specific role of childhood abuse, parental bonding, and family functioning in female adolescents with borderline personality disorder. *Journal of Personality Disorders*, 30(2): 177–192.

Izzo, A. A., & Ernst, E. (2009). Interactions between herbal medicines and prescribed drugs: An updated systematic review. *Drugs*, 69(13): 1777–1798.

Jain, R., Segal, S., Kollins, S. H., and Khayrallah, M. (2011). Clonidine extended-release tablets for pediatric patients with attention-deficit/hyperactivity disorder. *American Academy of Child and Adolescent Psychiatry*, 50(2): 171-179.

Jensen, P. S., & Kenny, D. T. (2004). The effects of yoga on the attention and behavior of boys with attention-deficit/hyperactivity disorder (ADHD). *Journal of Attention Disorders*, 7(4): 205-216.

Jiang, W., Li, Y., Du, Y., & Fan, J. (2016). Emotional Regulation and Executive Function Deficits in Unmedicated Chinese Children with Oppositional Defiant Disorder. *Psychiatry Investigation*, 13(3): 277-287.

Jonsdottir, I. H., Gerber, M., Lindwall, M., Lindegård, A., & Börjesson, M. (2013). The role of physical activity and fitness in prevention and treatment of mental health. *International Journal of Exercise Science*, 10(1): Article 72.

Joshi, K., Lad, S., Kale, M., Patwardhan, B., Mahadik, S. P., Patni, B., … Pandit, A. (2006). Supplementation with flax oil and vitamin C improves the outcome of Attention Deficit Hyperactivity Disorder (ADHD). *Prostaglandins, Leukotrienes, and Essential Fatty Acids*, 74(1): 17–21.

Kamp, C., F., Sperlich, B., & Holmberg, H. C. (2014). Exercise reduces the symptoms of attention deficit hyperactivity disorder and improves social behaviour, motor skills, strength, and neuropsychological parameters. *Acta Paediatrica*, Available online before publication. Doi: 10.1111/apa.12628.

Kay, G., Michaels, M., & Pakull, B. (2009). Simulated driving changes in young adults with ADHD receiving amphetamine salts extended release and atomoxetine. *Journal of Attention Disorders*, 12(4): 316-329.

Kessler, R., Adler, L., Barkley, R., Biederman, J., Conners, C. K., Greenhill, L. L., & Spencer, T. (2011). The prevalence and correlates of adult ADHD (p. 9-17). Chapter in *ADHD in Adults: Characterization, Diagnosis, and Treatment* (Buitelaar, J. K., Kan, C. C., & Asherson, P., Eds.). Cambridge, UK: Cambridge University Press.

Kessler, R. C., Adler, L., Barkley, R., Biederman, J., & Conners, C. K., et al. (2006). The prevalence and correlates of adult ADHD in the United States: Results from the National Comorbidity Survey Replication. *American Journal of Psychiatry*, 163(4): 716-723.

Kessler, R. C., Chiu, W. T., Demler, O., & Walters, E. E. (2005). Prevalence, severity, and comorbidity of twelve-month DSM-IV disorders in the National Comorbidity Survey Replication (NCS-R). *Archives of General Psychiatry*, 2005 Jun; 62(6):617-27.

Kiluk, B. D., Weden, S., & Culotta, V. P. (2009). Sport participation and anxiety in children with ADHD. *Journal of Attention Disorders*, 12(6): 499–506. http://dx.doi.org/10.1177/1087054708320400

Kingery, K. M., Narad, M., Garner, A. A., Antonini, T. N., Tamm, L., & Epstein, J. N. (2015). Extended visual glances away from the roadway are associated with ADHD – and texting-related driving performance deficits in adolescents. *Journal of Abnormal Child Psychology*, 43(6): 1175-1186.

Klein, R. G., Mannuzza, S., Ramos Olazagasti, M. A., Belsky, M. A., Hutchison, J. A., Lashua-Shriftman, E., and Castellanos, F. X. (2012). Clinical and functional outcome of childhood ADHD 33 years later. *Archives of General Psychiatry*, 69(12): 1295-1303.

Konstenius, M., Jayaram-Lindström, N., Guterstam, J., Beck, O., Philips, B., & Franck, J. (2014). Methylphenidate for attention deficit hyperactivity disorder and drug relapse in criminal offenders with substance dependence: A 24-week randomized placebo-controlled trial. *Addiction (Abingdon, England)*: 109(3): 440–9. doi:10.1111/add.12369

Lacy, J. W., & Stark, C. E. (2013). The neuroscience of memory: Implications for the courtroom. *Nature Reviews. Neuroscience,* 14(9): 649.

Lakes, K. D., & Hoyt, W. T. (2004). Promoting self-regulation through school-based martial arts training. *Journal of Applied Developmental Psychology*, 25(3): 283-302.

Larsson, H., Chang, Z., D'Onofrio, B., & Lichtenstein, P. (2013). The heritability of clinically diagnosed attention-deficit/hyperactivity disorder in children and adults. *Psychological Medicine*, 10:1-7.

Lazar, S. W., Kerr, C. E., Wasserman, R. H., Gray, J. R., Greve, D. N., Treadway, M. T., … Fischl, B. (2005). Meditation experience is associated with increased cortical thickness. *Neuroreport*, 16(17): 1893–7. Retrieved from http://www.pubmedcentral.nih.gov/articlerender.fcgi?artid=1361002&tool=pmcentrez&rendertype=abstract

Lenzenweger, M. F., Lane, M. C., Loranger, A. W., & Kessler, R. C. (2007). DSM-IV personality disorders in the National Comorbidity Survey Replication. *Biological Psychiatry*, 62(6): 553-564.

Lucke-Wold, B. P., Turner, R. C., Logsdon, A. F., Bailes, J. E., Huber, J. D., & Rosen, C. L. (2014). Linking traumatic brain injury to chronic traumatic encephalopathy: Identification of potential mechanisms leading to neurofibrillary tangle development. *Journal of Neurotrauma*, 31(13): 1129-1138.

Lundqvist, T. (2005). Cognitive consequences of cannabis use: comparison with abuse of stimulants and heroin with regard to attention, memory and executive functions. *Pharmacology Biochemistry and Behavior*, 81(2), 319-330.

MacIntosh, B. J., Crane, D. E., Sage, M. D., Rajab, A. S., Donahue, M. J., McIlroy, W. E., & Middleton, L. E. (2014). Impact of a single bout of aerobic exercise on regional brain perfusion and activation responses in healthy young adults. Published January 8, 2014 on *PLOSOne*.

Marquez-Castillo, R. L. (2014). *Martial Arts and ADHD: A meta-analysis*. Dissertation. Ann Arbor, MI: Walden University.

Mavilidi, M. F., Okely, A. D., Chandler, P., & Paas, F. (2016). Infusing Physical Activities Into the Classroom: Effects on Preschool Children's Geography Learning. *Mind, Brain, and Education*, 10(4): 256-263.

Mazereeuw, G., Lanctôt, K. L., Chau, S. A., Swardfager, W., & Herrmann, N. (2012). Effects of omega-3 fatty acids on cognitive performance: A meta-analysis. *Neurobiology of Aging*, 33(7): 1482-e17.

McCabe, S. E., Teter, C. J., & Boyd, C. J. (2006). Medical use, illicit use and diversion of prescription stimulant medication. *Journal of Psychoactive Drugs*, 38(1): 43-56.

McKnight-Eily, L. R., Eaton, D. K., Lowry, R., Croft, J. B., Presley-Cantrell, L., & Perry, G. S. (2011). Relationships between hours of sleep and health-risk behaviors in U.S. adolescent students. *Preventive Medicine*, 53(4): 271-273.

Mikulas, W. L. (2014). *Taming the Drunken Monkey: The Path to Mindfulness, Meditation, and Increased Concentration*. Woodbury, MN: Llewellyn Worldwide.

Minde, K., Eakin, L., Hechtman, L., Ochs, E., Bouffard, R., Greenfield, B., & Looper, K. (2003). The psychosocial functioning of children and spouses of adults with ADHD. *Journal of Child Psychology and Psychiatry*, 44(4): 637-46.

Miner, P. J. (2012). Melatonin for insomnia for children with ADHD. *Advance Healthcare Network*. July 27. http://nurse-practitioners-and-physician-assistants. advanceweb.com/Features/Articles/Melatonin-for-Insomnia-in-Children-With-ADHD.aspx

Ming, X., Mulvey, M., Mohanty, S., & Patel, V. (2011). Safety and efficacy of clonidine and clonidine extended-release in the treatment of children and adolescents with attention deficit and hyperactivity disorders. *Adolescent Health, Medicine and Therapeutics*, 2: 105.

Minnes, S., Singer, L. T., Min, M. O., Lang, A. M., Ben-Harush, A., Short, E., & Wu, M. (2014). Comparison of 12-year-old children with prenatal exposure to cocaine and non-exposed controls on caregiver ratings of executive function. *Journal of Youth and Adolescence*, 43(1): 53-69.

Mitchell, J. T., McIntyre, E. M., English, J. S., Dennis, M. F., Beckham, J. C., & Kollins, S. H. (2013). A pilot trial of mindfulness meditation training for ADHD in adulthood: impact on core symptoms, executive functioning, and emotion dysregulation. *Journal of Attention Disorders*.

Mitra, A., Pal, D., Minocha, M., & Kwatra D. (2010). Compatibility risks between drugs and herbal medicines or botanical supplements. *Toxicology Letters*, 196(1): S17.

Mohamed, L. A. E., Hanafy, N. F., & Elnaby, A. G. A. (2014). Effect of slow deep breathing exercise on blood pressure and heart rate among newly diagnosed patients with essential hypertension. *Journal of Education and Practice*.

Monica, D., Paulo, M., Appolinário, J. C., Freitas, S. R. D., Coutinho, G., Santos, C., & Coutinho, W. (2010). Assessment of executive functions in obese individuals with binge eating disorder. *Revista Brasileira de Psiquiatria*, 32(4): 381-388.

Molina, B. S. G., Hinshaw, S. P., Arnold, L. E., Swanson, J. M., Pelham, W. E., & Hechtman, L., et al. (2013). Adolesent substance abuse in the multimodal treatment study of attention-deficit/hyperactivity disorder (ADHD) (MTA) as a function of childhood ADHD, random assignment to childhood treatments, and subsequent medication. *American Academy of Child and Adolescent Psychiatry*, 52(3): 250-263.

Montgomery, P., Burton, J. R., Sewell, R. P., Spreckelsen, T. F., & Richardson, A. J. (2013). Low blood long chain omega-3 fatty acids in UK children are associated with poor cognitive performance and behavior: A cross-sectional analysis from the DOLAB study. *PloS One*, 8(6): e66697. doi:10.1371/journal. pone.0066697

National Osteoperosis Foundation. (2014). *Exercise for Strong Bones*. nof.org/articles/238

Nelson, J. M., Lindstrom, W., & Foels, P. A. (2014). Test anxiety and college students with attention deficit hyperactivity disorder. *Journal of Psychoeducational Assessment*, 32(6): 548-557.

Newcorn, J. H., Kratochvil, C. J., Allen, A. J., Casat, C. D., Ruff, D. D., Moore, R. J., Michelson, D., et al. (2008). Atomoxetine and osmotically released methylphenidate for the treatment of attention deficit hyperactivity disorder: Acute comparison and differential response. *American Journal of Psychiatry*, 165(6): 721-30.

Nock, M. K., Kazdin, A. E., Hiripi, E., & Kessler, R. C. (2007). Lifetime prevalence, correlates, and persistence of oppositional defiant disorder: Results from the National Comorbidity Survey Replication. *Journal of Child Psychology and Psychiatry*, 48(7): 703-713.

Nguyen, S., Nguyen, C., Chudnow, R., Miller, V., Riela, A., So, G., ... Shah, L. (2014). Efficacy of EPA Enriched Phosphatidylserine-Omega-3 (Vayarin) on Children with ADHD. *Neurology*, 82(10_Supplement): P.7-336. Retrieved from http://www.neurology.org/content/82/10_Supplement/P7.336.short

Onyike, C. U., & Diehl-Schmid, J. (2013). The Epidemiology of Frontotemporal Dementia. *International Review of Psychiatry (Abingdon, England)*, 25(2): 130–137. http://doi.org/10.3109/09540261.2013.776523

Overby, G. A., Snell Jr., W. E., & Callis, K. E. (2011). Subclinical ADHD, stress, and coping in romantic relationships of university students. *Journal of Attention Disorders*, 15(1): 67-78.

Pagoto, S. L., Curtin, C., Lemon, S. C., Bandini, L. G., Schneider, L. G., Bodenlos, J. S., & Ma, Y. (2009). Association between adult attention deficit/hyperactivity disorder and obesity in the U.S. population. *Obesity*, 17(3): 539–44.

Parswani, M. J., Sharm, M. P., & Iyengar, S. S. (2013). Mindfulness-based stress reduction program in coronary heart disease: A randomized controlled trial. *International Journal of Yoga*, 6(2): 111–117.

Pelham, W. E., Burrows-MacLean, L., Gnagy, E. M., Fabiano, G. A., Coles, E. L., Wymbs, B. T., Chacko, A., Walker, K. S., Wymbs, F., Garefino, A., Hoffman, M. T., Waxmonsky, J. G., & Waschbusch, D. A. (2014). A dose-ranging study of behavioral and pharmacological treatment in social settings for children with ADHD. *Journal of Abnormal Child Psychology*, 42: 1019-1031. doi:10.1007/s10802-013-9843-8.

Pietras, C. J., Cherek, D. R., Lane, S. D., Tcheremissine, O. V., & Steinberg, J. L. (2003). Effects of methylphenidate on impulsive choice in adult humans. *Psychopharmacology*, 170(4): 390-398.

Piper, B. J., Gray, H. M., Corbett, S. M., Birkett, M. A., & Raber, J. (2014). Executive function and mental health in adopted children with a history of recreational drug exposures. *PloS one*, 9(10): e110459.

Purushothaman, P. (2013). What's new with stimulants? *Child and Adolescent Psychopharmacology News*, 18(4):1-8.

Rascovsky, K., Salmon, D. P., Lipton, A. M., Leverenz, J. B., DeCarli, C., Jagust, W. J., ... & Galasko, D. (2005). Rate of progression differs in frontotemporal dementia and Alzheimer's disease. *Neurology*, 65(3): 397-403.

Raver, C. C., Blair, C., & Willoughby, M. (2013). Poverty as a predictor of 4-year-olds' executive function: New perspectives on models of differential susceptibility. *Developmental Psychology*, 49(2): 292.

Rietveld, M. J., Hudziak, J. J., Bartels, M., Beijsterveldt, C. V., & Boomsma, D. I. (2004). Heritability of attention problems in children: Longitudinal results from a study of twins, age 3 to 12. *Journal of Child Psychology and Psychiatry*, 45(3): 577-588.

Rommel, A. S., Halperin, J. M., Mill, J., Asherson, P., & Kuntsi, J. (2013). Protection from genetic diathesis in attention-deficit/hyperactivity disorder: Possible complementary roles of exercise. *Journal of the American Academy of Child and Adolescent Psychiatry*, 52(9): 900-910.

Ross, A., & Thomas, S. (2010). The health benefits of yoga and exercise: A review of comparison studies. *The Journal of Alternative and Complementary Medicine*, 16(1): 3-12.

Rusyniak, D. E. (2013). Neurologic manifestations of chronic methamphetamine abuse. *Psychiatric Clinics of North America*, 36(2): 261-275.

Sánchez-López, J., Fernández, T., Silva-Pereyra, J., & Martínez Mesa, J. A. (2013). Differences between judo, taekwondo and kung-fu athletes in sustained attention and impulse control. *Psychology*, 4(7): 607-612.

Sarkis, S., & Klein, K. (2009). *ADD and Your Money: A Guide to Personal Finance for Adults with Attention Deficit Disorder.* Oakland, CA: New Harbinger Publications, Inc.

Sawni, A. (2008). Attention-deficit/hyperactivity disorder and complementary/alternative medicine. *Adolescent Medicine State of the Art Reviews*, 19(2): xi, 313–326.

Schelleman, H., Bilker, W. B., Strom, B. L., Kimmel, S. E., Newcomb, C., Guevara, J. P., ... & Hennessy, S. (2011). Cardiovascular events and death in children exposed and unexposed to ADHD agents. *Pediatrics*, 127(6): 1102-1110.

Schuchardt, J. P., Huss, M., Stauss-Grabo, M., & Hahn, A. (2010). Significance of long-chain polyunsaturated fatty acids (PUFAs) for the development and behaviour of children. *European Journal of Pediatrics*, 169(2): 149–164.

Schwartz, S., & Correll, C. U. (2014). Efficacy and safety and atomoxetine in children and adolescents with attention-deficit/hyperactivity disorder: Results from a comprehensive meta-analysis and metaregression. *Journal of the American Academy of Child and Adolescent Psychiatry*, 53(2): 174-187.

Scott, J., & Freeman, A. (2010). Beck's cognitive therapy. In *Cognitive and Behavior Theories in Clinical Practice.* Edited by Kazantzis, N., Reinecke, M. A., & Freeman, A. New York: The Guilford Press.

Shanmugan, S., & Epperson, C. N. (2014). Estrogen and the prefrontal cortex: Towards a new understanding of estrogen's effects on executive functions in the menopause transition. *Human Brain Mapping*, 35(3): 847-865.

Shansky, R. M., & Lipps, J. (2013). Stress-induced cognitive dysfunction: Hormone-neurotransmitter interactions in the prefrontal cortex. *Frontiers in Human Neuroscience, 7.*

Shields, G. S., Sazma, M. A., & Yonelinas, A. P. (2016). The effects of acute stress on core executive functions: A meta-analysis and comparison with cortisol. *Neuroscience & Biobehavioral Reviews*, 68: 651-668.

Sikirika, V., Findling, R. L., Signorovitch, J., Erder, M. H., Dammerman, R., Hodgkins, P., Lu, M., Xie, J., & Wu, E. Q. (2013). Comparative efficacy of guanfacine extended release versus atomoxetine for the treatment of attention-deficit/hyperactivity disorder in children and adolescents: Applying matching-adjusted indirect comparison methodology. *CNS Drugs*, 27(11): 943-953.

Silvestri, R., Gagliano, A., Arico, I., Calarese, T., Cedro, C., Bruni, O., Condurso, R., Germano, E., Gervasi, G., Siracusano, R., Vita, G., & Bramanti, P. (2009). Sleep disorders in children with attention-deficit/hyperactivity disorder (ADHD) recorded overnight by video polysomnography. *Sleep Medicine*, 10(10): 1132-1138.

Sinn, N., Bryan, J., & Wilson, C. (2008). Cognitive effects of polyunsaturated fatty acids in children with attention deficit hyperactivity disorder symptoms: A randomised controlled trial. *Prostaglandins, Leukotrienes, and Essential Fatty Acids*, 78(4-5): 311–26.

Sinn, N., & Bryan, J. (2007). Effect of supplementation with polyunsaturated fatty acids and micronutrients on learning and behavior problems associated with child ADHD. *Journal of Developmental and Behavior Pediatrics*, 28(2): 82–91.

Smalley, S. L., Loo, S. K., Hale, T., Shrestha, A., McGough, J., Flook, L., & Reise, S. (2009). Mindfulness and attention deficit hyperactivity disorder. *Journal of Clinical Psychology*, 65(10): 1087-1098.

Smith, J. M. (2015). *Genetic and Environmental Influences on Executive Functioning 12 Months After Pediatric Traumatic Brain Injury* (Doctoral dissertation, University of Cincinnati).

Snitselaar, M. A., & Smits, M. G. (2014). Sleep, Melatonin, and Circadian Rhythmicity in Attention Deficit Hyperactivity Disorder. In *Melatonin and Melatonergic Drugs in Clinical Practice*, (pp. 379-384), Springer India.

Solanto, M. V. (2012). "CBT for ADHD: An interview with Mary Solanto Ph.D." Stephanie Sarkis, PhD, "Here, There, and Everywhere" *Psychology Today* blog. https://www.psychologytoday.

com/blog/here-there-and-everywhere/201210/
cbt-adhd-interview-mary-solanto-phd

Spann, M. N., Mayes, L. C., Kalmar, J. H., Guiney, J., Womer, F. Y., Pittman, B., ... & Blumberg, H. P. (2012). Childhood abuse and neglect and cognitive flexibility in adolescents. *Child Neuropsychology*, 18(2): 182-189.

Stanos, S., Brodsky, M., Argoff, C., Clauw, D. J., D'Arcy, Y., Donevan, S., ... Watt, S. (2016). Rethinking chronic pain in a primary care setting. *Postgraduate Medicine*, 128(5): 502–515.

Strand, M. T., Hawk Jr, L. W., Bubnik, M., Shiels, K., Pelham Jr, W. E., & Waxmonsky, J. G. (2012). Improving working memory in children with attention-deficit/hyperactivity disorder: The separate and combined effects of incentives and stimulant medication. *Journal of Abnormal Child Psychology*, 40(7): 1193-1207.

Streeter, C. C., Whitfield, T. H., Owen, L., Rein, T., Karri, S. K., Yahkind, A., Perlmutter, R., Prescot, A., Renshaw, P. F., Ciraulo, D. A ., & Jensen, J. E. (2010). Effects of yoga versus walking on mood, anxiety, and brain GABA levels: A randomized controlled MRS study. *Journal of Alternative and Complimentary Medicine*, 16(11): 1145-1152.

Strimas, R., Davis, C., Patte, K., Curtis, C., Reid, C., & McCool, C. (2008). Symptoms of attention-deficit/hyperactivity disorder, overeating, and body mass index in men. *Eating Behaviors*, 9(4): 516–518.

Surman, C. B. H., Hammerness, P. G., Pion, K., & Faraone S. V. (2013). Do stimulants improve functioning in adults with ADHD?: A review of the literature. *European Neuropsychopharmacology*, 23(6): 528-533.

Taylor, A. F., & Kuo, F. E. (2009). Children with attention deficits concentrate better after walk in the park. *Journal of Attention Disorders*, 12(5), 402-409.

Thomas, C. (2013). Extended release alpha-2 agonists for ADHD. *Child and Adolescent Psychopharmacology News*, 18(2): 7-9.

Travis, F., & Shear, J. (2010). Focused attention, open monitoring and automatic self-transcending: Categories to organize meditations from Vedic,

Buddhist and Chinese traditions. *Consciousness and Cognition*, 19(4):1110–1118.

Trick, L. M., & Toxopeus, R. (2013). How missing a treatment of mixed amphetamine salts extended release affects performance in teen drivers with ADHD. Proceedings of the Seventh International Driving Symposium on Human Factors in Driver Assessment, Training, and Vehicle Design. http://www.drivingassessment.uiowa.edu/sites/default/files/DA2013/Papers/016_Trick_0.pdf

Treuer, T., Gau, S. S., Méndez, L., Montgomery, W., Monk, J. A., & Altin, M., et al. (2013). A systematic review of combination therapy with stimulants and atomoxetine for attention-deficit/hyperactivity disorder, including patient characteristics, treatment strategies, effectiveness, and tolerability. *Journal of Child and Adolescent Psychopharmacology*, 23:179-193.

Twomey, S. (2010, January). "Phineas Gage: Neuroscience's most famous patient." *Smithsonian Magazine*.

U.S. Department of Health and Human Services, Office of Disease Prevention & Health Promotion. (2012). *Physical Activity Guidelines for Americans Midcourse Report: Strategies to Increase Physical Activity Among Youth*. http://www.health.gov/paguidelines

Van der Oord, S., Bögels, S. M., & Peijnenburg, D. (2012). The effectiveness of mindfulness training for children with ADHD and mindful parenting for their parents. *Journal of Child and Family Studies*, 21(1): 139-147.

Van Egmond-Fröhlich, A. W. A., Weghuber, D., & de Zwaan, M. (2012). Association of symptoms of attention-deficit/hyperactivity disorder with physical activity, media time, and food intake in children and adolescents. *PloS One*, 7(11): e49781.

Van Ittersum, K., & Wansink, B. (2012). Plate size and color suggestibility: The Delboeuf Illusion's bias on serving and eating behavior. *Journal of Consumer Research*, 39(2): 215-228.

Van Veen, M. M., Kooij, J. J., Boonstra, A. M., Gordijn, M., & Van Someren, E. J. (2010). Delayed circadian rhythm in adults with attention-deficit/hyperactivity disorder and chronic sleep-onset insomnia. *Biological Psychiatry*, 67(11): 1091-1096.

Vaughan, B., Fegert, J., & Kratochvil, C. J. (2009). Update on atomoxetine in the treatment of attention-deficit/hyperactivity disorder. *Expert Opinion on Pharmacotherapy*, 10(4): 669-676.

Viola, T. W., Tractenberg, S. G., Pezzi, J. C., Kristensen, C. H., & Grassi-Oliveira, R. (2013). Childhood physical neglect associated with executive functions impairments in crack cocaine-dependent women. *Drug and Alcohol Dependence*, 132(1): 271-276.

Wagner, D., Becker, B., Koester, P., Gouzoulis-Mayfrank, E., & Daumann, J. (2013). A prospective study of learning, memory, and executive function in new MDMA users. *Addiction*, 108(1): 136-145.

Wang, M. Y., & An, L. G. (2011). Effects of 12 weeks' tai chi chuan practice on the immune function of female college students who lack physical exercise. *Biology of Sport*, 28(1): 45-96.

Warren, A. E., Hamilton, R. M., Bélanger, S. A., Gray, C., Gow, R. M., Sanatani, S., ... & Miles, B. (2009). Cardiac risk assessment before the use of stimulant medications in children and youth: A joint position statement by the Canadian Paediatric Society, the Canadian Cardiovascular Society, and the Canadian Academy of Child and Adolescent Psychiatry. *Canadian Journal of Cardiology*, 25(11): 625-630.

Van de Weijer-Bergsma, E., Formsma, A. R., de Bruin, E. I., & Bögels, S. M. (2012). The effectiveness of mindfulness training on behavioral problems and attentional functioning in adolescents with ADHD. *Journal of Child and Family Studies*, 21(5): 775-787.

Weiss, M. D., Wasdell, M. B., Bomben, M. M., Rea, K. J., & Freeman, R. D. (2006). Sleep hygiene and melatonin treatment for children and adolescents with ADHD and initial insomnia. *Journal of the American Academy of Child & Adolescent Psychiatry*, 45(5): 512-519.

Wigal, S. B., Emmerson, N., Gehricke, J. G., & Galassetti, P. (2013). Exercise: Applications to childhood ADHD. *Journal of Attention Disorders*, 17(4): 279-290.

Wilens, T. E. (2004). Attention-deficit/hyperactivity disorder and the substance use disorders: The nature of the relationship, subtypes at risk, and treatment issues. *Psychiatric Clinics of North America*, 27(2): 283–301.

Wittchen, H. U., Mhlig, S., & Pezawas, L. (2003). Natural course and burden of bipolar disorders. *International Journal of Neuropsychopharmacology*, 6: 145-54.

Witte, A. V., Kerti, L., Hermannstädter, H. M., Fiebach, J. B., Schreiber, S. J., Schuchardt, J. P., ... & Flöel, A. (2013). Long-chain omega-3 fatty acids improve brain function and structure in older adults. *Cerebral Cortex*, bht163.

Woo, H. D., Kim, D. W., Hong, Y. S., Kim, Y. M., Seo, J. H., Choe, B. M., Park, J. H., Kang, J. W., Yoo, J. H., Chueh, H. W., Lee, J. H., Kwak, M. J., & Kim, J. (2014). Dietary patterns in children with attention deficit/hyperactivity disorder (ADHD). *Nutrients*, 6(4): 1539–1553.

Wood, B., Rea, M. S., Plitnick, B., & Figueiro, M. G. (2013). Light level and duration of exposure determine the impact of self-luminous tablets on melatonin suppression. *Applied Ergonomics*, 44(2): 237-240.

Yan, W. S., Li, Y. H., Xiao, L., Zhu, N., Bechara, A., & Sui, N. (2014). Working memory and affective decision-making in addiction: A neurocognitive comparison between heroin addicts, pathological gamblers and healthy controls. *Drug and Alcohol Dependence*, 134: 194-200.

Young, G. S., Conquer, J. A., & Thomas, R. (2005). Effect of supplementation with polyunsaturated fatty acids and micronutrients on learning and behavior problems associated with child ADHD. *Reproduction, Nutrition, Development*, 45(5): 549–558.

Youssef, N. A., Ege, M., Angly, S. S., Strauss, J. L., & Marx, C. E. (2011). Is obstructive sleep apnea associated with ADHD? *Annals of Clinical Psychiatry* 23(3): 213-224.

Zhao, Y. Y., Zhang, S. Q., Wei, F., Fan, Y. M., Sun, F., & Bai, S. (2014). Quality control of natural product medicine and nutrient supplements 2014. *Journal of Analytical Methods in Chemistry*, Epub ahead of print.

Zylowska, L. (2012). "ADHD and mindfulness: An interview with Lidia Zylowska M.D." Stephanie Sarkis, PhD, "Here, There, and Everywhere" *Psychology Today* blog. https://www.psychologytoday.com/blog/here-there-and-everywhere/201206/adhd-mindfulness-interview-lidia-zylowska-md

Zylowska, L., Ackerman, D. L., Yang, M. H., Futrell, J. L., Horton, N. L, Hale, T. S., Pataki, C., & Smalley, S. L. (2008). Mindfulness meditation training in adults and adolescents with ADHD: A feasibility study. *Journal of Attention Disorders*, 11(6): 737–46.

Made in the USA
Columbia, SC
21 March 2023

14092444R00109